THE LAST GUIDE'S GUIDE
(to family, money, fishing
and everything else
that matters)

OTHER TITLES BY RON CORBETT

The Gatineau

The Last Guide: A Story of Fish and Love

One Last River Run

The Rideau Canal: Then and Now

A Grand Adventure:
America's First Transcontinental Truck Run

First Soldiers' Down

THE LAST GUIDE'S GUIDE

(to family, money, fishing and everything else that matters)

RON CORBETT

OTTAWA PRESS AND PUBLISHING

OTTAWA
PRESS AND
PUBLISHING

ottawapressandpublishing.com

ISBN 978-1-988437-00-2 (pbk.)
ISBN 978-1-988437-01-9 (epub)
ISBN 978-1-988437-02-6 (mobi)

Copyright © Ron Corbett 2016

Photography: Julie Oliver
Cover design: Scott Sigurdson
Interior design, typesetting and graphics
(vignettes on section pages after photos by Julie Oliver):
Magdalene Carson / New Leaf Publication Design

Cataloguing in Publication data
available at Library and Archives Canada

In Memory of
Robert Corbett
and
Rhonda Corbett

The Lessons

Contents

Preface

The Last Guide's Guide is a book of things Frank Kuiack considers important and how to do most of them. Frank is the oldest fishing guide in Algonquin Park.

The book began the year Frank needed surgery on his eye. He was seventy-six at the time. It was his left eye that went bad on him and although nothing proved long-term or calamitous there was no way of knowing that at the time and it left Frank thinking he should make a record — of good lakes he knew; how to fish proper; things that worked and things that didn't — before he went blind.

Maybe, that was more my idea. Certainly it has always struck me as a good idea. To record what Frank knows.

Frank is the last of a generation of fishing guides and bushmen that once flourished in the Algonquin Highlands, a region in north-central Canada that will always be special to me as Algonquin Park is where I spent most summer holidays as a child. Many in Canada and the United States can say the same, and I suspect with the same fond memories.

Although it started with urgency *The Last Guide's Guide* took four years to complete. It was written over seven fishing trips. When we were done, Frank said we had been working on the book long enough to have earned a university degree and maybe we'd been in a classroom these past four years instead of a canoe. I thought that was a fine way of looking at it.

Year One

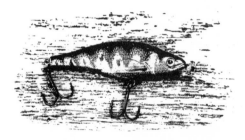

If I ever go looking for my heart's desire again, I won't look any further than my own back yard. Because if it isn't there, I never really lost it to begin with.

— L. Frank Baum, *The Wonderful Wizard of Oz*

Anyone can be a fisherman in May.

— Ernest Hemingway, *The Old Man and the Sea*

The bad-eye incident — A boy-doctor — The last cooper — Driving through the Algonquin Highlands — Whitney

In mid-December of 2011 Frank Kuiack awoke with a sore eye. It was his left eye, and he rubbed at it, blinked, rubbed at it again but the eye remained sore. He lay in bed trying to remember if he had done anything to the eye — splashed it, poked it — but nothing came to him.

When he got out of bed and stood he was surprised to discover his vision was blurry as well. Not up close or mid-distance, mind, and not far-away all the time, but throughout the morning and at times of the day afterwards that he could never tell were about to come upon him, Frank couldn't see.

He was in Cornwall when this happened, visiting his daughter for Christmas, and because of this Frank didn't say anything. Figuring he would be a distraction. Figuring he was visiting family and there was probably no need to see great distances anyway.

When he was back home, he waited three months for the eye to heal. Began to compensate by walking at an angle. Approaching objects from the left-hand side. Driving with his bad eye closed and rotating his head to make up for his loss of peripheral vision.

More than one person in Whitney, Ontario, the small village where Frank lived, had told him they'd seen him driving down Highway 60 the other day and, my Lord, what was you doing, Frankie?

"What do you mean?"

"Gawd, you wuz twistin' your head back and forth like some damn fool bobble head."

"Bobble head?"

"Yeah, some damn fool bobble head. Or maybe there was some hornet trapped in the truck with you. But it's March. So I figure you wuz a bobble head."

"Wuz you drinkin'?"

When the questioning became too much for Frank he went to see a doctor. It was a young doctor who had just opened a practice in Pembroke, a ninety-minute drive from Whitney. The doctor shone a light into Frank's eyes and then started twisting his head around to get a good look inside.

After doing that the doctor started tut-tutting. He was dressed in a white lab-coat that didn't seem to fit him and a stethoscope that hung too low on his neck. Frank thought it strange, that a boy would be standing in front of him tut-tutting.

"You should have come to see me right away, Mr. Kuiack," the doctor said. "Don't know if we could have caught it in time, but there's no sense dragging these things out. This must be painful, isn't it?"

"A bit."

"Yes, I would imagine. You're going to need surgery I'm afraid."

"It's that bad?"

"Bad enough. But completely treatable. You shouldn't worry."

Which worried Frank. Although not for reasons you might expect. Frank had spoken only Polish before being sent to Whitney Public School and of all the English words the boy was soon to learn, the word "shouldn't" would prove to be one of the more problematic.

Shouldn't was a word that didn't stand up straight, it seemed to Frank. Always hesitant and unsure of itself. Why, the list of shouldn'ts Frank had been warned about and gone ahead and done anyway was long and ongoing and there seemed to be no consequence to most of it.

None of which he told the boy-doctor, choosing to say instead:

"What 'bout my other eye?"

"I suspect you're going to have problems there before long as well, Mr. Kuiack."

"Could I go blind cause of all this?"

"You shouldn't."

———◆———

Frank drove home from Pembroke wondering if he could work as a one-eyed fishing guide.

He thought he would be all right in a canoe, and for most of the stuff you had to do in the bush, but could you drive in Ontario if you only had one eye? The government seemed to be sticklers about eyes. The one thing they tested you on each time you renewed your licence.

Had Frank ever seen a man wearing an eye-patch sitting behind a steering wheel?

He kept thinking. Driving through the mixed hardwood and pine forests that lay to the south of Algonquin Park; the village of Round Lake Centre, with a community centre in the middle of town where Frank remembered going to barn dances in the '50s and '60s.

He cut through Wilno, Canada's oldest Polish settlement, where he was born in 1935, then through the villages of Barry's Bay and Madawaska. Not long after that he was back in Whitney.

As he pulled into his driveway it still hadn't come to him: the memory of a one-eyed man behind a steering wheel.

He headed to his basement door, thinking his bad eye might be more of a problem than he had first thought.

————◆————

The next day Frank phoned me. The call came early Tuesday evening, when I was preparing school lunches and about to take the dog for an evening walk. There was an hour-or-so worth of work to do in my study when I came back from the walk. Frank's call was a welcome break from this nightly routine and I sat at the kitchen table to talk to him.

I believe the first thing he said after I sat down was:

"I think I'm going blind."

"You're what?"

"Goin' blind. Or half-blind. I don't know. I can't see out my left eye."

"When did this happen?"

"Few months back."

"Have you done anything about it?"

"Went to a doctor yesterday. I'm goin' to need surgery."

"So it's serious. But the surgery will take care of it, right?"

"Don't know. The doctor is twelve years old."

While Frank talked, I stared around the kitchen. At my wife finishing the children's sandwiches, the dog sitting by the door, our backyard, almost in darkness but you could see the last mounds of snow, the white fence around a patch of mud that would be a vegetable garden in two months. Spring was just about here.

Then my eyes passed over the stack of newspapers in our recycling bin. On top of the pile was a news story about a wooden-barrel maker from England. I reached over to grab the newspaper.

Now that's odd.

Frank at his "office," a rotary telephone and fish-fillet table by his back door. People leave handwritten messages for him on butcher's paper.

———◆———

As Frank kept talking about his bad eye — the doctor said he was going to pop the eye right out, like a Life Savers, Frank could watch if he wanted on a television in the operating room, would you ever want to see a thing like that? — I glanced at the newspaper.

The story was about the last wooden-barrel maker in England — you're called a cooper when you do that — and the last cooper was looking for an apprentice. His name was Alastair Simms and he had started searching a few years back, when he learned he was the last one.

Hadn't realized he was the last one until someone told him. He had been working away, making wooden barrels, doing his job, when one day he looked up and every other cooper had disappeared.

The same thing had happened to Frank. He was working as a fishing guide in Algonquin Park, when one day he looked up and every other guide had gone.

The world around him had changed too. Algonquin Park was no longer a destination for rich American anglers but now for working families that started arriving in the '60s with rental canoes, foam coolers and Red Devil spinners purchased at a Canadian Tire store the day before.

After that, being a fishing guide in Algonquin Park was like being Big Foot. Something people reported seeing from time to time but most thought couldn't exist.

A few years ago, Frank was down to a handful of repeat customers: some Mennonite farmers from London, Ontario who used to lease a cabin on Canoe Lake. A taxidermist, from Maynooth. Some dentists from Ohio; so enfeebled on their last visits that they arrived with canes and walkers. Frank finally told them they didn't need him anymore, they should fish from the highway. He'd show them some spots.

What made him keep going? What made Alastair Simms keep going? The stories were identical right down to the questions left behind.

Strangest thing about the news story was that I had read it two months ago.

————◆————

"I had to to cancel all my clients for May," I heard Frank say. "Some people are not too happy with me right now."

As Frank talked I waved the newspaper at my wife and mouthed, "where did this come from?" She shrugged her shoulders and mouthed back, "I don't know."

This newspaper should have been thrown out weeks ago. We live in a city with bi-weekly garbage pick-up. We never miss things.

There was an awkward pause on the telephone and I realized I had lost track of the conversation.

"So when can you go fishing, Frank?" I asked.

"I don't know. That's what I been tryin' to tell ya."

"No idea whatsoever?"

"None. I'm stuck at home waitin' for a phone call from the doctor."

The face of the last cooper stared out at me. Next to a pull quote that read: "I'm going to keep working as a master cooper until I'm dead but I'm very keen to pass on my knowledge."

————◆————

A month later I was on my way to Algonquin Park. I told Frank I had already booked time off work so I might as well come. Maybe he could teach me some things while I was there. If his bad eye kept us from fishing.

He asked what sort of things and I said I'd explain when I got there, although the honest answer right then would have been — I'm not sure.

I had met Frank twelve years earlier, while writing a story for the *Ottawa Citizen* about wolves in Algonquin Park. I interviewed him because he was a municipal councilor at

Whitney, Ontario in the late 1930s

the time, and during the interview learned he was also a fishing guide in Algonquin Park.

The story on the wolves appeared in the *Citizen* that September. The following month a much longer story on Frank was published. A year later the feature had been turned into a book, *The Last Guide*, published by Penguin Books Canada.

The Last Guide told the story of Frank's life and I am as amazed at that story today as I was then. How he started guiding at the age of eight, after some fishermen camped on Galeairy Lake asked if he could row them around and show them the good spots. Frank was paid more for an afternoon fishing then his father made in a week at a St. Anthony Lumber bush-camp.

You tend to notice something like that. So Frank kept guiding. For what would have been, at that time, the next fifty-seven years.

He came from a family of eighteen children and had thirteen children and stepchildren himself. Went to school for five years. Worked as a guide at Hay Lake Lodge and Long Lake Lodge and helped take down the Highland Inn, although he never worked at that fabled Inn, something he has always regretted.

As well as guiding he worked in bush-camps, removed road kill in Algonquin Park, sold firewood, shoveled driveways and did whatever else he needed to do to keep living in the Algonquin Highlands and be available for fishing trips, when someone wanted to hire him.

He was a bad drunk for many years but stopped drinking in his 50s. Goes to an AA meeting every Wednesday night at the United Church in Whitney. Has his AA pins on display on a wall of his living room, next to a photo of his wife and a stuffed brook trout.

A good story, but a dozen years down the road I felt a twinge of writer's remorse. *The Last Guide* described the action in Frank's life, but never asked why he had done all that, or what he had learned and come to believe by doing all that.

In that time I had come to believe Frank had a unique way of looking at the world. A world-view completely of his making and that left him — somehow, strangely, how does he do that? — a contented person.

So much so I once told my wife that the happiest people I've met as a journalist are not rich and powerful people; not popular and gifted people. They are retired people who have looked after their money. And Frank Kuiack.

Frank was his own category. Maybe I had missed a better story.

————◆————

The boy rowed the boat across Galeairy Lake. He was just tall enough to see over the gunnels, his arms just long enough to reach the oars, and so the boat tracked a crooked path across the water.

He lived in a farm on the eastern shore of the lake and was on his way to Whitney, to get the mail for his mother. The fastest way to reach the village was by boat. Along the way the boy stopped in a bay not far from where the Madawaska River flowed out of the lake, and fished.

The boy's family owned only one boat. Getting the mail was the only time he could use the boat and he always made sure to fish when he had that chore. He had a wire line with him, spooled around a thick stick; some store-bought hooks one of his brothers had given him, and a bucket of frogs.

He stayed in the bay twenty minutes. Caught three black bass and threw them all back. He was hoping there might be speckle trout by the mouth of the river but as normally happened, he caught only bass.

He beached the boat and went to the post office, in the back room of Doctor Cannon's home. The boy went to the back door and waited while the doctor's wife went to get the mail.

Mrs. Cannon was baking that morning and there was flour in her hair, which she had tied back in a bun, but a few strands had broken free. When she handed over the mail she talked to the boy and blew strands of hair away from her face. The boy thought it an amazing trick.

"Ned says he has a couple days' work around the house, if you dad was interested. Can you tell him?"

The boy nodded.

"Your dad or one of your brothers. Dominique did a nice job on the pantry."

The boy nodded again. He spoke only a few words of English but understood it all right. He took the bundle of mail and headed back to the boat.

Before he got there two men approached him. They were dressed in heavy wool clothing and boots with so much metal, it reminded the boy of work tools. A tall man and a short, fat man. It was the tall one who spoke.

"You caught some nice fish on your way in, son," he said. "Do you live around here?"

The boy pointed across the lake. You couldn't see his farm but there was smoke coming from the chimney, rising through the pine.

"I see. Well, you would know this lake quite well then, wouldn't you?"

The man's voice inflected up as though he were asking a question but the boy wasn't sure. Of course he would know the lake.

The men had been sitting in front of a tent when the boy came ashore. There were always men camped on the shores of Galeairy Lake in the spring and summer. Men who dressed in strange clothing and spoke in sing-song voices, who came from somewhere called "the States," according to his father.

The boy had no idea where that was. Only knew the men arrived every year to fish for black bass.

"Are you in a hurr,y son?"

That sounded like more of a question, although the boy still didn't know how to answer. He was never in a hurry. Not that he knew. Unless hurry meant something different than running around not thinking about stuff, which is what he thought it meant.

Maybe it meant something different.

"We were wondering if you could take us fishing," the man continued. "Show us some of the good spots."

Now that was a question. Although again, a strange one. Why would he go fishing with these men? His mother was waiting for the mail. He had chores to do after that.

"Gotta go," said the boy, and he started to walk to the boat.

"Are you sure? We can pay you," said the man.

The boy kept walking.

"We have money."

The boy stopped. When he turned around the man was pulling from his pocket a bundle of paper money thicker than an Eaton's catalogue. More money than the boy thought was possible to have in just one pocket.

"We'll pay for the rental of your boat as well," the man said.

The boy started walking back.

———◆———

The drive from Ottawa to Algonquin Park hasn't changed much in the years that I have been making it, going back to when I was a young boy sitting in the backseat of my father's car.

There are four lanes on the Trans-Canada Highway heading to Arnprior (although not beyond, despite a four-lane highway to Pembroke being a political promise dating back to the days of Diefenbaker.)

Highway 60 in autumn, just south of Whitney

There is an ugly mish-mash of gas stations, fast-food restaurants and cloverleaf ramps at the intersection to White
Lake. Ownership of the Golden Sands restaurant at Golden
Lake has changed hands a few times. The village of Wilno
has three restaurants.

I remember a black bear in a cage outside a souvenir
shop and gas station that we would stop to see whenever
I came as a child, can't remember where exactly, which is
strange as a black bear in a cage outside a souvenir shop
and gas station is the sort of thing you would expect to stay
with you. But the bear is gone.

The rest of the drive is pretty much the same. Change
comes slowly to the Algonquin Highlands, never embraced
but accepted grudgingly it seems, like offering a bed to an
alcoholic uncle trying to get back on his feet, knowing even
as you hold open the door that this is probably not going
to end well.

The Algonquin Highlands, part of the much larger Lau-
rentian Highlands, were formed eleven thousand years ago
when a glacier travelled through, gouging out rivers, lakes,
bluffs, escarpments and leaving behind rocky hills, giant
pine, and a valley the size of the United Kingdom where
there had once been a great sea.

While the valley and the river running through it — the
Ottawa Valley and the Ottawa River — have played pivotal
roles in Canadian history, the Algonquin Highlands have
been pivotal to nothing.

Woodland Indians such as the Ojibwa and Algonquin
used the Highlands for fishing and hunting but never
settled here. No great battles were fought there. No grand
habitations built. When Europeans arrived in the mid-19th
Century they found the land inhospitable to farming and
of no military or political importance.

Indeed, the land was considered so worthless it couldn't
even be given away. A settlement road started by the

government of Upper Canada in the 1850s to entice people to the Highlands was abandoned long before its final destination at Opeongo Lake. It was the only colony road in Ontario people fled from.

———◆———

Whitney is five kilometres from the eastern border of Algonquin Park. Coming from Ottawa, you first see the village when cresting a hill overlooking the Madawaska River and it is laid out rather nicely for you in the valley below.

You can see a post office and liquor store, next to a hockey rink and community centre. The Freshmart grocery and Algonquin Lunch Bar are nearby, closer to the Madawaska River. On the east side of the river is a bank, a pizza parlour and the Twin-E restaurant.

On the west side, heading toward Algonquin Park, is the East Gate Motel, Opeongo Outfitters, Maochullo's Garage, and on a clear day you might even see the Ontario Provincial Police station on the edge of town.

On the Madawaska River proper you will see three resorts, including one large, all-seasons couples' resort once called Bear Trail Inn, until some years ago the owner decided clarity was a virtue and changed the name to The Couples Resort.

After you have taken in all of that you have taken in all of Whitney.

The actual population of the town is not posted on the highway sign, but according to the 2011 census the population of South Algonquin Township — which includes the villages of L'Amable, Aylen Lake, Cross Lake, Gunters, Madawaska, McKenzie Lake, Murchison, Opeongo, Wallace and Whitney — was 1,211.

Which was down forty-two people from the 2006 census.

———◆———

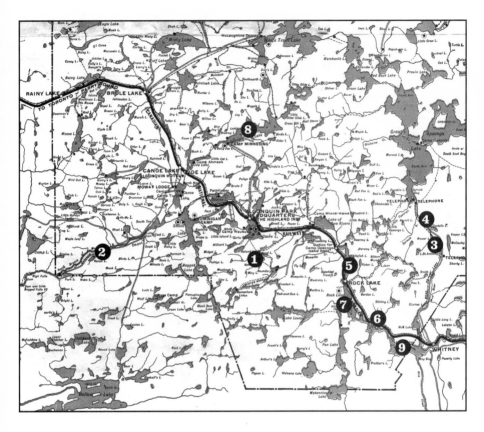

Lakes and rivers fished in the *Last Guide's Guide*
(*Excerpt from a 1922 Canadian National Railways map of Algonquin Park*)

1 Head Lake	**4** Costello Lake	**7** Rock Lake
2 Oxtongue River	**5** Whitefish Lake	**8** Burnt Island Lake
3 Brewer Lake	**6** Aubrey Lake	**9** Galeairy Lake

Frank lives not far from the Couples Resort, in a house you reach by turning off Highway 60, then going up a street lined with hardwood trees, down another tree-lined street until you reach a bluff on the highest point of the street, and there you find a house almost hidden behind ten-foot cedars.

The first time I drove through those cedars and down Frank's laneway I thought I had entered another world. It was no different twelve years later.

When I arrive I count eleven boats in Frank's backyard. It would have surprised me if two could float. There are canoes with holes in the beam and aluminum fishing boats missing keels, some so badly rusted the original metal is now some previously unknown and unimagined earth-tone colour.

There are barrels filled with water and outboard motors in the barrels, clamped to wooden crossbeams, ready to be tested. I stare at the barrels and wonder how many busted-up outboard motors a man needs to own before he sets up a testing facility.

There is a vegetable and herb garden behind a freshly painted picket fence. A garage and work-shed that had been built in stages across the back of the yard, three distinct stages, built when Frank had assembled the necessary money and parts to continue, the middle stage having a roof made from a Marlboro billboard. A cowboy smoking a cigarette: sitting on top of Frank's garage each morning to greet the sun.

"Come on up, door's open," I hear him yell from inside the house.

———◆———

I take out my bag and head toward the basement door, along the way passing a fish-fillet table Frank has built by the door. There is a rotary phone on the wall above the table, a roll of brown butcher's paper at one end, knives, batteries and pails beneath. Frank's office, some have joked.

When I come through the basement door I walk past a minnow tank and several cube freezers, up stairs lined with Nescafe coffee jars and rain slickers hanging from wall pegs. At the top of the stairs I walk into Frank's kitchen, where I find him sitting at a table, doing a word-puzzle book.

"You're late," he says.

"Sorry. Had trouble getting out of the city."

Frank is wearing a hat so large I can't see his face. The rest of Frank looks unchanged from when I last saw him: dark-green pants and shirt. Plaid slippers. A Buckmaster knife on his belt. A cup of coffee near one hand, his other reaching for a pouch of tobacco.

But there is no face.

"What's with the hat?"

"It's to keep people from starin' at my bum eye," he says, going on to explain he had to start wearing an eye-patch a few weeks ago and after that everyone started asking him questions about his eye, some people asking if they could touch the patch, so he figured he would distract people by wearing a hat. Frank believes people will always look at a man's hat if he goes through the effort and bother of putting one on his head.

Or at least he always does. But do you know what, Ron?

"What, Frank?"

"People don't do what they should in this world."

"They kept starin' at your eye?"

"Every last one of 'em."

"So what did you do?"

"Went out and bought bigger hats."

I'm not sure if it was a sad expression that crossed his face right then. Certainly it was a sad-seeming nod of the hat atop his head: a double-winged, Australian bushman's hat.

"That didn't work out either I'm betting."

"Nope. Seems a one-eyed man is always going to get looked at in this world. I had no idea. It's almost rude. Staring at a man with a bum eye. Like runnin' circles around a man with only one leg."

"I hadn't thought of it that way."

"Well you wouldn't. You got two good eyes."

"So whadda think? Speckles or lakers?"

Frank has made us supper: grilled chicken thighs and boiled potatoes, cut cucumber and early beets from a neighbour's vegetable garden. We are sitting at his kitchen table.

His surgery has been scheduled and cancelled twice, so he has gone back to guiding. If the doctor's aren't taking the eye seriously, he doesn't see why he should.

"Either one," I answer. "It's been a hot month. Still doing well with the speckles?"

"Holy Jeepers yes. My nephew is catching' 'em right out of the culvert on Brewer Lake. Not even puttin' in a canoe."

"Speckles would be fun."

"Lakers are good right now too."

"What do you feel like?"

"Feel like trollin' I think."

"So lakers?"

"We could go to Head Lake. They been bitin' real good in there this year."

"We've fished Head before, haven't we?"

"We have. You caught a couple."

"Let's go back there then."

"Good."

We wash the dishes, make cups of instant coffee and when we are back at the table Frank says:

"So what did you want me to teach you?"

"How to be a better fisherman."

A guide carrying packs for a fishing trip
in Algonquin Park, circa 1890s

"Holy Jeepers. How much time do ya t'ink I got?"

"Thanks. But I was thinking of other things as well. You've talked about it yourself in the past. How you'd like to record a few things, about Algonquin Park, about fishing, before you ... you know," and I point at his eye-patch.

"'Fore I can't fish anymore."

"You're the one who mentioned it."

"Well, I was thinkin' 'bout it. You're right. I'm going to have kids around here one day that maybe I won't be able to take out anymore. Maybe I should record some stuff while I still can."

I go to the spare bedroom where I had put my bag, take out the newspaper story about the last cooper. Go back to the kitchen table.

"What's this?" Frank asks when I hand him the newspaper.

"A story that was staring me in the face when you called the other day."

———◆———

When Frank finishes reading, he says:

"That sure sounds familiar."

"Doesn't it though."

"So you want to be my apprentice?"

"We don't have to go that far."

"What was you thinkin'?"

"Why don't I start recording some of our conversations. We can put together a record that way. We'll do it while we're fishing."

Frank doesn't say anything right away. As though considering it.

"If we're going to do it we should start soon," I say.

"'Cause I'm seventy-six and wearing an eye-patch?"

"That's not a bad reason. Here's another one — you really are the last guide, Frank. Not the last one working anymore.

The last one, period. When I was driving up I started thinking about it. The other guides I interviewed twelve years ago, the ones I could find; they're all gone, aren't they?"

Frank doesn't say anything for a minute.

"Walter's gone," he says eventually.

"Yes he is. Same with Felix Luckasavitch. Neil Sawyer. There's no one left but you."

"Which means what?"

"Means I'm going to ask you some questions when we go fishing tomorrow."

◆2◆

Fishing for lake trout — The Lost Boys — The Twin E restaurant gets a new wall clock — A shore lunch — The problem with fish finders — Visiting the Madawaska Bait and Tackle Shop

I awake the next morning to the sound of Frank's alarm clock. He has a Westinghouse model from the '50s, solid metal, with a steel tine that hits a brass bell like some steroid-crazed boxer. Although Frank's bedroom is halfway across the house, the alarm is loud enough for me to think it's under my pillow.

I groan, remembering the sound of that clock. I open my eyes and look at my watch: 4:30 a.m.

I throw my legs out of bed, get dressed and walk to the kitchen, where I find Frank standing next to the sink, buttering toast. A bowl of cereal has already been poured for me.

"Kettle's hot," he says.

"Are the thermoses already made?"

"Right on."

I make a cup of instant coffee and sit down to eat my cereal.

"I'm anxious to get going," I say. "I didn't go fishing at all last year."

"Not once."

"No."

Frank with one of his salvaged canoes

"Were you sick?"

"No, just busy at work."

"Well, there's somethin' it'd be easy to teach you. Don't do that again."

———◆———

The gear was left out the night before, so when we finish breakfast we just clean our dishes, grab the rucksacks and fishing rods and make our way to the basement. At the bottom of the landing the minnow tank glows in the dark like a kid's night-light.

Frank walks outside with little fish shadows moving across his back.

We load his van in the darkness, pull out of the laneway and start to drive through Whitney, our headlights the only light to be seen except for a yellow bulb burning behind the Algonquin Lunch-Bar, just strong enough to light up parts of the dam at the end of Galeairy Lake.

We turn onto Highway 60 and can hear the Madawaska River but not actually see it. Same for the hills surrounding us. We know they're there, can sense them, but not see them. It must work like cabin pressure.

We pass Opeongo Outfitters. The OPP station. Two minutes later we are in Algonquin Park.

———◆———

Algonquin Park is more than 7,500 square kilometres in size, or roughly one-and-a-half times that of Prince Edward Island. The Ontario government established the park in 1893, eight years after the creation of Banff National Park (Algonquin was called a national park until 1913.)

It is one of the longest portages in Algonquin Park to get into Head Lake. Nearly 1,700 metres, starting from the south shore of Cache Lake.

Because Frank has twenty-three canoes stashed at lakes around Algonquin Park, it is nothing more than a pleasant hike for us. We beach his motorboat at the trailhead to the portage — after travelling down Cache Lake in near darkness, only a false-dawn light from a sun hiding in the trees but not yet risen — grab our rucksack and fishing rods and begin walking.

When Frank goes off to get the canoe I sit on a rock to wait and the sun clears the tree-line. The tallest branches of the spruce ringing the lake light up like the tips of burning cigarettes for a minute. I hear grey jays for the first time and small animals moving somewhere in the forest behind me.

When Frank comes paddling into view I groan for the second time that day.

Although I long ago quit asking questions about the seaworthiness of any of Frank's boats — figuring I'm going to go fishing with him anyway so why bother asking questions — it still comes as a shock sometimes. What I am expected to crawl into. With the expectation it will float.

Frank rarely buys a boat. Each canoe has been given to him or rescued from a dump somewhere and later repaired. Fishing boats have normally been pulled from the bottom of lakes. Found in abandoned bush-camps. Scrap-metal yards.

The canoe today is a rotten-lettuce-green colour. With a band of duct tape around the middle of the beam. It has a ragged edge that reminds me of suture scars.

"Nice boat."

"Thanks. You gettin' in?"

———◆———

Lake trout belong to the Salmonidae family, which has three distinct genera, nearly two-dozen species, and an almost infinite number of subspecies and hybrids. Every fish in the family is considered to be a game fish, some being the most sought-after in the world.

You can find lake trout — the second-largest fish in the salmonidae family; only the Chinook salmon is larger — in 150 lakes in Algonquin Park. Which is twenty percent of all lake-trout lakes in Ontario.

Trout are a cold-water fish and the Algonquin Highlands are paradise for cold-water fish. When that glacier travelled through eleven thousand years ago, the melting ice it left behind was trapped in the Highlands. Warm-water fish like bass and pike were trapped outside, unable to scale the crown of land the glacier had left behind.

For its first fifty years most visitors to Algonquin Park were sports fishermen. "Sports" as the fishing guides used to call them. They came from Southern Ontario and the United States and stayed at lodges in the Park, the most famous being the Highland Inn, built on Cache Lake by the Grand Trunk Railway in 1908.

Each of the Sports came in the hope of catching not only trout, but record trout. In those days *Field and Stream Magazine* had an annual list of the biggest fish caught in North America and it was a rare year that didn't have a lake trout or speckle trout from Algonquin Park on the list. Lake of Two Rivers made the list several times, as did Cache Lake, Rock Lake, Opeongo Lake and the Oxtongue River.

That retreating glacier didn't do the Highlands many favours — left behind a bedrock of gneiss and granite, thin top-soil, rocky hills and un-navigable rivers — but that cold water almost made up for it.

———◆———

You catch lake trout today pretty much the same way you did in 1893. You troll for them. Using short rods and heavy reels and steel line in the old days. You paddle around a lake with a lure running behind the canoe, looking for trout depth, or "trout water" as it is often called, the depth where a school of some of the most magnificent fresh-water fish

Fishing for trout in Algonquin Park, circa 1890

in the world might be swimming right beneath your canoe.

It is a lazy form of fishing. You never cast. Never work a fly across the top of the water.

Until you catch a fish, you paddle around a lake and don't do much more than talk.

———◆———

"You brought a tape recorder?"

"I did. My phone actually, but I have a microphone."

"So whadda want to ask me?"

"What do you think we should start with?"

"Well, fishing would be a good thing to know."

"All right, let's start there. What's the most important thing to know about fishing?"

Frank considers it for a minute and then says:

"You gotta know where the fish are. Don't matter what else you're doin', if you ain't in the right place, you ain't goin' to catch fish."

"So how do you know where the fish are?"

"You just gotta know. There's a shoal there where speckles hang out. It's August so the lakers are going to be real deep. You gotta know stuff like that."

"What about fish finders?"

"They'd be good for you. I use 'em all the time. Problem there, is people start to rely on 'em too much."

"What do you mean?"

"Well, bass fisherman, tournament bass fisherman, that's what they do all the time. Use fish finders. They got 'em set to bing whenever they find a fish."

Frank has finished rolling a cigarette and taken out his Zippo lighter.

"So that's what they do all day — run around a lake chasing bings. They never stay anywhere to work anything."

He is spitting tobacco flakes into the water.

"Fish finders are good, but they ain't as good as knowin' what you're doin'."

———◆———

We troll by the western shore of Head Lake, working a channel of deep water where Frank normally catches lakers. The shoreline is pine and cedar for the most part, a flat shoreline with no cliffs or escarpments, as you often find on lakes in the Park. The only cliffs are at the end of the lake, near a set of waterfalls coming in from Kenneth Lake.

We troll for close to two hours without any luck. The day starts to warm and before long we have taken off our sweaters. The clouds are mid-cumulus, cartoon-looking clouds, like the ones you see on the opening credits of *The Simpsons*.

A bull moose comes to the shore near where we are fishing and just stands there watching us, never doing anything more than that, not moving so much as a muscle that we can see, leaving after ten minutes without once taking a drink of water or turning his eyes away.

Frank says the cow is probably hiding nearby with the calf and now that we have passed inspection we might even see them later. They will come walking down to the shoreline all high-limbed and gangly and probably head to the rushes on the south shore. He had seen moose there a few times before.

Whenever you see a bull by a lake this time of year, assume the family is nearby. Don't approach him. More than one tourist in Algonquin Park, fishing in the spring or early summer, has gone to get a closer look at a bull moose standing on the shoreline not doing anything at all, as if dazed, perhaps injured, and has found out soon enough the animal is not injured. Plenty of energy left.

———◆———

"You never told me what you thought of Walter," says Frank, as we continue trolling. He is referring to Walter Sawyer, one of the guides I interviewed years ago.

Frank and friends showing off fishing trophies

"Bit of a character."

"Lawd, you got that right. Where'd you meet him?"

"At his house."

"That garage next to his daughter's?"

"That was the place."

"He probably told you he were a better fisherman than me."

"He did."

"Probably wanted his own book."

"He may have suggested that."

Frank starts laughing. He may have suggested that. If he knew Walter Sawyer, and he did, the suggestion would have been made the minute I walked into his home. Frank asks me.

"He actually suggested it on the phone, before I went over."

Frank starts slapping his knees. There is a big smile on his face. It was fun, talking again about Walter Sawyer.

———◆———

Every guide I've met, at least the ones from Frank's generation, had a certain Lost Boys quality to them. Frank was showing it right then. They often seemed to be young boys trapped inside old men's bodies. Mischievous and boastful. Playful and adventurous. To a man I suspected they would be happiest if they could stay outside and never come home for supper.

They competed against each other constantly. I've thought about that over the years. Why does every Hollywood movie and current novel depict people who live and work outdoors — commune with nature is the phrase most often heard — as wise, soft-talking, Great-Spirit-communing heroes? When I've only met rowdy Lost Boys from Peter Pan?

The guide I spent most time with, other than Frank, was Walter Sawyer. He was a few years older than Frank and had been the head guide at Hay Lake Lodge. Which made him Frank's boss for many years, something Frank thought was neither logical nor natural. The exact opposite: a nonsensical aberration.

I interviewed Sawyer in his home and as soon as I walked through the door he presented me with a wolf's tooth, telling me if I wanted another one for my son or daughter that wouldn't be a problem because he knew how to get wolf's teeth. Not many people did.

When I was sitting down he asked why I was doing a book on Frank, "when I'm sittin' right here in front of you?" I glanced at a cane in the corner of the room and asked Sawyer when he had last guided. He snorted and said:

"What difference would that make? It's not like I've forgotten how to do it. I never forget anything."

———◆———

Frank keeps talking about fishing, how to do it properly: "Some guys never use worms 'cuz they think it's kid's stuff. That's stupid. Worms catch fish."

And how to do it poorly:"If you cast upriver you're an idiot."

I am not listening to the "dispassionate dissemination of information." I am listening to boasts, opinions, a little teasing — wrapped around information.

It is instruction from a Lost Boy. Who wants it clearly understood: I'm better at this than anyone else you're going to meet today.

———◆———

The competition between Frank and Walter Sawyer went back and forth for years, each man having his moments of triumph and defeat, although it may have been Frank who had the last laugh. The opportunity presented itself the day the owner of the Twin-E restaurant approached him and said she was having a problem with Walter.

"What's the problem?" asked Frank.

The owner, who was well aware of the antipathy between the two men and was counting on this to make sure nothing got back to Walter, replied that she didn't mind Walter coming to the restaurant. She wanted that clearly understood. What she minded was Walter sitting at the lunch counter. Talking to her all morning. Talking to her customers all morning.

It was news-of-the-day stuff for the most part. Same-sex marriage. Immigration. The conspiracy that is ethanol. Walter had opinions on just about any news topic, and if the discussion ever turned to a topic he was unfamiliar with, why, he was such a quick study that he was sure to have a strong opinion pretty soon.

"I don't mind what he says," explained the owner, "I just don't want him at the centre of everything. He should sit at a table like everyone else. The counter is for people in a hurry."

Frank thought about the problem for a minute. Decided against pointing out the obvious. No one in a hurry ever went to the Twin E Restaurant. Said instead:

"So you don't mind Walter being in the restaurant. You just don't want him sitting at the counter, by the cash register, is that right?"

"That's right."

"I think I can help you."

Frank went home. Looked for the Christmas gift one of his nephews had given him the year before. Found it in a box and returned to the restaurant.

"Try this," he said to the owner, handing over the box. "Hang it on the wall behind the cash register. I betcha that'll solve your problem."

The next morning when Walter arrived at the Twin E he ordered his coffee, shouted hello's to the men already sitting at the tables in back and another hello to the cook, who poked his head out the kitchen window to say hello back, which didn't normally happen.

When Walter had done all that he took a sip of coffee, put down the cup, looked up and saw a wall clock with Frank's face. The words *Last Guide* written underneath. Frank was smiling at Walter and letting him know it was 9:45 a.m.

Walter didn't return to the Twin E for two weeks. Some thought it longer but no one thought to start timing him when he walked out of the restaurant so it was a matter of debate at the Twin E for some time but little more.

Walter never sat at the counter again. Always at whatever open table was furthest from the cash register. Nor can anyone recall him looking at the wall clock ever again, and while most thought this was because of Frank's face being there, a few of the regulars, these tending to be of a more reflective and retiring nature, saw something much more profound in Walter's actions.

These men argued that the shock of seeing Frank's face on the clock had simply left Walter no longer caring about time.

———◆———

By late morning we move off the western shore and start trolling the entire lake. Right down the middle. By the waterfalls coming in from Kenneth Lake.

It is near the waterfalls that we catch our first fish. A small laker, caught by Frank, and when he brings it in the boat he whoops lik a boy on the midway. The fish has the fine grey and green colouring of a lake trout. A deep vee-notch in the tail.

"There we go," he says, looking at his fish-finder at the same time. "They're at thirty feet, passing right in front of the waterfalls."

We put the fish on a stringer and continue trolling.

It was hard not to laugh at Frank when he caught that fish, a man in his 70s whooping with joy at catching a two-pound lake trout, a fish he has caught — well, what would it

Frank showing trout caught on a fishing trip
out of Hay Lake Lodge, mid-'60s

be? Thousands of times? Tens of thousands of times?

The fish didn't matter much. So long as it's a fish and that means he doesn't have to go home and tell people he "got skunked," which when Frank says it are two of the saddest, loneliest words you're ever going to hear.

Whatever else fishing may be, it is competition.

Loving competition puts Frank out of step with the times in many ways. A thought that occurred to me when I saw him catch the first fish of the day.

Certainly we are discouraging it in our children. Imagining a different future.

Some school districts have dispensed with grades for elementary students, saying it is a passé form of competition. Some amateur soccer games are now played without keeping score. Sports tournaments are held without awarding prizes or trophies. I had done a story on such a tournament just the month before.

Today, many adults consider competition to be as socially acceptable for children as nose-picking or sticking your tongue on the monkey bars in February.

I have described Frank's overall demeanor as that of a young boy. Perhaps the words I should be using are "old fashioned."

Frank catches another lake trout a few minutes later, a bigger fish this time, you can tell by the bass-clef curve to his rod. By the sound of the steel line coming in, not smoothly this time, but with a clickety-clack, clickety-clack sound to it.

The fish dives a few times and Frank plays his rod around the canoe, making sure it doesn't come up under the boat, or worse, jump the other side of it. Lakers don't often jump, but you never know.

Ten minutes later the fish is in the net. Not as big as it seemed at first, but three pounds, maybe three-and-a-half. A big fat belly. A fish that could feed a family of four. When the Ontario government started stocking lakes in the Highlands more than a century ago that was the primary reason given. So people living here would have something to eat.

Twenty minutes later, still trolling by the waterfalls, I catch my first fish of the day, another small laker, about two pounds, and Frank says we should go for our shore lunch.

———◆———

A shore lunch, prepared by your fishing guide, was always part of the service in the hey-day of guiding in Algonquin Park. Quite often lunch had as much to do with the tip a guide got at the end of the day as the number of fish that were caught.

To Frank, a shore lunch is something sacred. Not to be messed with. Not to be changed. You are insulting him, and throwing off his rhythm, if you ever try to help. You are expected to watch and be impressed.

By how quickly your guide starts the fire. How quickly he fillets the fish. How he seasons it with powder he keeps in a pouch attached to his belt, or if not on his belt than some place never far from sight.

Sometimes he will gather plants from the forest to add more flavour to the fish. If young boys are in the fishing party, he will fashion them balsam boats and send them off to play.

He will do all this in less than fifteen minutes. Present you with a plate of fried fish, cooked beans and buttered toast, a coffee pot placed in the embers of the fire already starting to burble.

It is serious stuff to this day. Frank has a secret batter recipe for his fried fish. There is only one hand-written copy of the recipe and it is in his safety-deposit box. His will bequeaths the recipe to his daughter, Adele.

Frank gets the store-bought ingredients for his recipe at different groceries, to make it more difficult for people to figure out. In case he is ever followed.

I once made a joke, while sitting in his kitchen, that I might be able to figure it out just by looking at his spice rack. Next time I returned to Whitney, the spice rack was gone.

———◆———

Frank fillets the first laker he caught and cooks it over a fire he has burning in only a few minutes. He serves the fish with sliced cucumbers and dinner rolls and we sit across the shore from the waterfalls, eating our lunch with plates upon our knees.

We watch a couple of fishermen who have come to the lake, trolling down the south shore, where we had no luck most of the morning. Frank watches them for a few minutes and says:

"You'd almost think they knew what they were doin', fishin' right there."

"Maybe they do."

"Nah, did you see that one guy's tackle box?"

"I did. He's carrying it in the dry-sack."

"It's 'bout half the size of the dry-sack. You don't need anything near that big. Stupid carryin' that much weight."

He goes to the canoe and brings back his tackle box, little more than a small Tupperware container. He sits down beside me, takes five lures from the box and says:

"I'm stupid too, 'cause these are the only lures you'll ever need."

"For trout?"

"For anythin'."

Then he thinks for a minute.

The Five Lures You'd Be an Idiot Not to Own

After seventy years of fishing in Algonquin Park, Frank has tried every trout and bass lure on the market. Here are the five lures he will always take with him on a fishing trip.

From top to bottom:

1. **Rapala Husky Jerk**: A classic trolling lure, great for lake trout, pickerel, pike and bass.

2. **Mepps Black Fury, Number 2:** Probably the most popular spinning lure on the market. A great lure for speckle trout and smallmouth bass

3. **Arbogast Hula Popper:** Frank's go-to surface lure. Great for largemouth bass and pike.

4. **Cotton Cordell Big O**: First verifiable, million-selling lure. Also first square-lip crank-bait brought to market. If you're a bass fisherman, you have this lure.

5. **Williams Wabler**: One of the most popular trolling lures of all time, invented right in Algonquin Park. Great for lake trout.

(Note: Although manufacturers' names are given for the lures, this list is not product placement. Editors suggested removing the company names but Frank told them: "It makes a difference," and so they remain.)

"Unless you're going for musky. Which is stupid no matter what you're usin'."

———◆———

We record more interviews after lunch. Although he moves quickly while preparing the meal, Frank is never in a hurry to go back fishing. This was something that surprised me at first, until I realized it was all part of the rhythm, to a good day spent fishing.

When the dishes are washed Frank will drink a coffee and smoke a cigarette. Talk about how the fishing was that morning. What it might be like that afternoon.

He will talk about the formation of the clouds in the sky, and what that might mean for the weather. Talk about the portage out or where to pitch camp that night.

Sometimes he will have a short nap.

Starting with this fishing trip, it is now also the time when I turn on the microphone and he answers questions.

———◆———

The fishing cools for us after lunch. Frank already has his limit, but I can take one more out, so we troll for a while by the waterfalls, than try the south shore one more time.

In a couple hours, when the sun has reached its high point, Frank says we might as well head out. Frank pretty much organizes his fishing days around the sun. Be on the lake before you see it. Leave before it drops. It keeps the days organized.

On the drive back to Whitney he says he has a few errands to run before he goes home and we head to Paradise Road, on the other side of Galeairy Lake from Frank, where Kevin Heinz lives. He is a conservation officer at Algonquin Park and one of Frank's closest friends.

When he answers his door, Frank hands Heinz one of the trout he caught that day, still on the stringer.

Getting trout delivered to his front door does not seem to surprise him.

"What lake were you at?" he says.

"Head."

"Nice laker. I'll start up the barbecue."

"Can't stay. We're driving down to see Matt. Thought you might like the trout."

"Too big just for me. Have a bite on your way back if you can."

————◆————

We drive to the village of Madawaska next, where Matt Fitzpatrick has opened a bait-and-tackle store. Fitzpatrick moved to Madawaska after his father was diagnosed with cancer, deciding after that happened that he would quit drinking and try to be there for his dad.

Fitzpatrick was living in Niagara Falls at the time, working at a hotel that gave bar-discount coupons to its employees and as Matt's children were grown and had left home, he was free to use the coupons most days.

After he gave up drinking, his father's cancer went into remission and Fitzpatrick believed his sobriety had something to do with it. Maybe not a direct cause-and-effect relationship. Maybe something more along the lines of karma, or setting the right mood for good things to happen. But there was an obvious connection.

Matt's good actions had been rewarded. His father had beaten cancer. The decision to quit drinking and take charge of his life — give it purpose, quit drifting along — had been the right decision to make and maybe he needed to make more such decisions.

The next spring Matt divorced his wife, moved to Madawaska and opened a bait store.

"It's a good bait shop," says Frank, carrying a bucket of minnows and a Tupperware case of whitefish tails into the Madawaska Bait and Tackle shop (which was actually a garage next to the house where Matt was renting an apartment, a hand-painted sign nailed to a maple in the front yard letting you know there was a bait-and-tackle shop in the garage).

"Just about out of white-fish tails, Frank," says Fitzpatrick when we walk into the garage. "Hope you brought some."

"Two cases."

"Great. Don't know if I need more minnows. You can't use them in the Park."

"I know that. Can use 'em everywhere else. You can have what I brought. I got too many right now as t'is."

"Well ... I'll take them then. Thanks, Frank."

On our way back to Whitney, Frank says it was going to be a challenge, keeping the Madawaska Bait and Tackle store open. But he felt up to the challenge.

"It's prit' near a scandal," he said. "Not having a good bait and tackle shop in Madawaska."

————◆————

Frank used to see the other guides in town. Some came right to his house, to buy moonshine from his father. Basil Sawyer came often. Joe Lavally, a guide so famous he had a book written about him, came often.

He would see Lavally bass fishing on Galeairy Lake sometimes. With a boatload of Sports from one of the inns in Algonquin Park.

The Sports would whoop and cheer whenever they caught a fish. Slap Lavally on the back and make toasts to him. Frank wondered how that would feel. He was the youngest boy in a family of eighteen and most days it was hard to even get noticed.

His brother Edmund, when he returned in the spring from the bush-camps, would tease him about wanting to be a fishing guide.

"You been guidin' again, Frankie?" he would ask his kid brother.

"Every day this week."

"What are the Sports payin' you?"

"Depends how many fish we catch."

"Whadda mean it depends how many fish you catch? Don't you have a flat rate?"

Frank looked embarrassed and stammered: "They pay me at the end Edmund. No one has ever given me less than four dollars."

"Four dollars? You know how much a guide makes at the Highland Inn? Ten dollars a day. That's the flat rate. Some guys make more. Do people know how much you're chargin'?"

"What do you mean?"

"The other guides. They know you workin' with no flat rate?"

"Jumpin' Edmund, I don't talk to none of the guides. How would I ever talk to them?"

"You think maybe they talk to some of the Sports you been guidin'?"

Frank didn't say anything. Just stared at his older brother, trying to look sure of himself, the way his father had looked the day he threw a drunken Sport over the Madawaska Dam for not stepping aside.

"You be careful," said Edmund. "Some of those old boys would just as soon cut ya up and use you for bait as they would spit in your eye."

The next day Frank told the first group of Sports to approach him — when he had rowed his boat across the lake to the tent city where the Sports lived each spring and summer — that he had a flat rate of five dollars a day. And they couldn't tell anyone about it.

He also wanted them to consider, and here he struggled to say the word, even though he had practiced saying it with Edmund the night before, giving him great choo-ities.

"Sorry, Frank?"

"Great choo-ities. You maybe, should give me some of those too."

Frank's tackle box

"Gratuities?"

Frank nodded his head. Gave the Sport a stern, I mean-business look, which he had also practiced with Edmund the night before.

"Yes, well, not a problem. We normally pay you five dollars, do we not? And if we have success in battle today, no problem with a gratuity. Are you ready to go?"

Frank nodded and gave the Sport a pail of frogs. Kept a stern look on his face, not sure when he should stop doing that. Edmund hadn't actually said.

LESSON TWO
Why You Should Fish

"I had a friend once, name of Jim Holly. He had the franchise rights to Arby's for all of New York State. Lived in Buffalo. A rich man. Met him when I was guidin' at Hay Lake.

"When Hay Lake closed he still came up to fish and I'd always guide him. He was a big man. Loved to hunt as well. Then one year he had a stroke and got paralyzed on the right side. It came back some, his movement, but his face was froze on that side and he was never right again.

" (A few years after the stroke) he invited me to his home. I'd been there a few times but not recently. It was a mansion, this big old house Jim lived in. He was in a wheelchair and I don't think he was much bigger'n me by that time.

"His wife served us coffee and left us in his study. All Jim wanted to talk about was Algonquin Park. What the fishin' had been like that year, how I had done, askin' me to describe some of the trips I'd been on. He closed his eyes one time when I was doing that and I knew he was 'imaginin' it.

"That March Jim killed himself. Took one of his huntin' rifles and in that room we had been sitting in he blew his brains out. People have a lot of reasons to go fishin'. For me, I think you should fish so you can stay right thinking in this world."

✦ 3 ✦

Fishing the Oxtongue River — Tom Thomson — Picking Chaga mushrooms — Champlain versus Cartier — How to belong somewhere — Taking down the Highland Inn

Frank's eye surgery took place the middle of July. His left eye was popped out, three rather nasty cysts were removed, his right eye was thoroughly inspected while he was there on the operating table, then he was given prescription ointments and new eye patches and sent home.

When I came back to Whitney in mid-August he was still wearing the patch and would do so until the end of the month. After that his eye looked swollen and bruised for a while but he could see out it all right. By Christmas, the eye was about back to what it had been.

———✦———

While I waited to return to Whitney I started transcribing some of the interviews from Head Lake. Why you should fish. The five fishing lures you'd be an idiot not to own. Plants that are useful and how to spot them.

Before leaving Whitney, Frank said maybe the "recordings" we were making could be turned into "a guidebook or something." I asked him what he thought should be in a good guidebook and he said: "Practical stuff people can use. Not the stupid stuff."

As I read the transcribed interviews, I thought he would be pleased. It occurred to me his answers to some of the questions were close to short lessons.

——————◆——————

I didn't get out of Ottawa as early as I had hoped and the sun was barely in the sky on the day I returned to Whitney. As I drove down Frank's street, I was surprised to see that some of the leaves on the soft maples had started to turn. There were brown pine needles blowing across the road.

I found him sitting at his kitchen table, doing a word-puzzle book, my supper sitting on a plate at the other end of the table.

"You're late."

"Came as fast as I could."

"Traffic bad?"

"No, I was just late getting away from work."

I ate supper and watched television as Frank made coffee. The television was turned to a fishing channel, the sound turned down, some men fishing from a jet boat in what looked like the Florida Keys. Frank likes watching people fish but doesn't like to listen to them. I have watched the fishing channel many times while sitting at his kitchen table but have never heard the sound.

When he turns up the volume on his television, normally he has it tuned to a country-music station in the 900s. Over the years I have grown to like Lefty Frizzell. Hank Snow. Kitty Wells.

"So what do you wanna fish for?" he asks, when I have finished washing the dishes and made myself a cup of coffee.

"Can we go for speckles this time?"

"Sure we could."

"It's not too late in the season?"

Frank at home, doing word-puzzles at his kitchen table

"Bit trickier, but there's a few places we can try."

"What about the Oxtongue?"

"Jeepers, you'd almost be out of the Park. We don't have to go that far."

"But if we did, would we catch any?"

"Oh yeah. I know some good spots on that river. I got a canoe stashed at Tea Lake."

"By the dam?"

"That's right. Guess we could leave the van in the parking lot they got there."

He hesitated. Frank prefers fishing lakes to rivers and I knew that was the main reason. But the Oxtongue is a beautiful meandering river; with some stretches so narrow you can reach your hands out from your canoe and touch alders and chokeberry bushes on both shorelines. Deep pools of water on just about every lazy-bend.

Fly fisherman love the river, including the painter Tom Thomson, who fished it regularly. One of the most famous photos ever taken of Thomson has him standing on the Tea Lake Dam, fly rod in hand, casting into the Oxtongue River.

"I don't mind going a little further," I say. "If you're all right with it."

"All right. Oxtongue River it is."

———◆———

Frank's alarm goes off the next morning at 4:30 a.m., which surprises me. I thought he would adjust for the extra distance to the Oxtongue. I have got up as early as four to go fishing with Frank.

I get dressed quickly but when I walk into the kitchen I find Frank screwing the cap onto a thermos of coffee. There is the smell of fried eggs in the air but the frying pan is drying in the rack beside the sink.

"We'll have breakfast on the way," he says, handing me a fried-egg sandwich wrapped in butcher's paper. There's the adjustment.

For the longest time I didn't understand why Frank started the fishing day so early. It rarely seemed worth it. The first hour on a lake was generally slow, nothing happening until the sun popped over the trees and the mist started to burn off the water.

I have no memory of catching fish in the dark.

I asked him about it one day and he said I was probably right. Not a lot of "action" at the start of the day. But it was still important to get out there early. So we'd be there when the fish were ready.

Only later in the day did it occur to me that I had just heard a complete reversal of the traditional angler-fish relationship. I always assumed we were leaving early because that's when the fish would be waiting. Frank left early so he could be there waiting, when the fish were ready.

———◆———

Frank's headlights have no trouble picking up the highway signs on Highway 60 as we drive through the Park that morning. The light-refracting signs seem to jump out at us from the darkness. The Algonquin Logging Museum. Opeongo Lake. Killarney Lodge. Lake of Two Rivers Campground. Bartlett Lodge. The turn-off to Arowhon Pines Resort. Canoe Lake. Tea Lake.

We are almost at the west gate of the Park when we see a sign for the Oxtongue River picnic ground. We turn off the highway and drive past the picnic ground, the sound of a river running beside us though we can't see it. We take a switch-back road to a small dam.

By the time we reach the Tea Lake dam the sun has come out but has not yet risen. It is hiding on the other side of the trees, a glow coming through the forest that resembles the cook-fires of a travelling army. It will be another twenty minutes or so before it clears the tree-line.

Frank goes to find his canoe while I unload the van. I stare at the rocks below the dam, one large one in particular,

Tom Thomson fishing the Oxtongue River

halfway across the river, wondering if rocks that size get swept away in the spring. Or do they stay there for a hundred years?

———◆———

By most accounts Tom Thomson wasn't a great guide. He was a southern Ontario boy who came to the Highlands, learned how to catch trout, than hung out a shingle at Mowat Lodge. Guide for hire. The one year he had an actual guide's licence, 1917, the Park Superintendent misspelled his name.

But he looked the part. The photo of Thomson fishing the Oxtongue River shows him wearing a toque and heavy-cloth work-shirt, breeches and sturdy looking mid-calf moccasins. He has a fishing rod in his right hand and is standing almost jauntily on a rock in the middle of the river, white water rushing past him.

Good guide or not, in that photo Thomson looks like someone who belongs in the Algonquin Highlands. Show anyone a photo of *The Jack Pine* — Thomson's most famous painting — then show them the Tea Lake Dam photo and I don't think a person on the planet would say: "No, I can't imagine it. That man being the painter of Jack Pine."

Everyone would see the connection. Thomson belonged in the Highlands. An artist who, if he were not destined to paint The Jack Pine, was certainly destined to paint something pretty close to it.

Belonging somewhere is not as simple as you may think. There is more to it than being born, never moving, and then dying. That could mean you belonged in the place you lived, but could also mean you were timid and feared change. Which would be something different.

Just like Thomson, Frank belongs in the Algonquin Highlands so perfectly he might as well be a geographic feature. Some map coordinate. You don't often meet people like that today, where we are either blessed or cursed with rampant individualism, unprecedented independence, limitless travel and access to just about anything we want, anytime we want it.

Every day, it seems, we can wake up and decide to be someone else. Doing something else. Someplace far away. Many ad campaigns are built upon the untethered life.

And every day most people wake up and can't decide what to become. Spend the day considering their options. As though clicking their way through Netflix.

Frank never has to waste time on such things. Next Wednesday he will be unlocking the door of the United Church in Whitney for the weekly AA Meeting. The last Saturday of April, opening day of trout season, he will be fishing. Next year he will be living in the Algonquin Highlands.

———◆———

Tom Thomson died in 1917. His body was found drifting on Canoe Lake eight days after he went missing. There have been many different theories about his death, which likely would have amused Thomson, a man who hated artifice and embellishment, who inspired the artists that would later form the Group of Seven when he started painting what he saw in front of him, nature as it presented itself, not romanticized or re-arranged in his head.

Frank had heard all the theories, as had everyone in the Highlands. Thomson had been murdered by poachers. Or by a disgruntled guide who thought Thomson was a poseur. Maybe it was suicide. Then his body was stolen. Or maybe it was never his body. Thomson had orchestrated his own disappearance.

A lot of theories and Frank didn't believe any of them. He was of the opinion that the most pedestrian of explanations for Thomson's death was the likeliest. He capsized his canoe while taking a piss. Hit his head and drowned.

He'd known another guide who had died the same way.

————◆————

The sun clears the trees just as we are putting the canoe in the water. Over the tree-line of Tea Lake the sky brightens, then the light skips over the dam and lights up the Oxtongue River. A sudden shower of orange and yellow light rolls down the river as though it is something material.

We take our first paddle strokes with the river lighting up in front of us. The alder bushes come out of the shadows, along with chokeberry, stunt-pine and balsam. If we were a hundred miles south, the vegetation would be willows and maples. In the Highlands, the banks of meandering rivers are covered by thorn bushes and dwarf trees.

We don't travel far down the river before we start fishing. There are four portages on the Oxtongue, along with a few bridges, culverts and other easily recognizable physical features. Frank asks that I don't get too specific about where we are fishing.

"There are a few spots in here that are gold," he explains. "Long time ago I took a friend of mine to one of the best ones. Rest of that summer, every time I came back here, I'd find him fishing that same spot. I don't know if he ever moved off it.

"By the end of the summer the fish were gone. I asked him why he ruined it for everyone and he said he couldn't help himself. Knowing he was guaranteed to catch speckles in that spot, he couldn't stay away. He said it was worse than a drug. He lost interest in everything else. Got fat that summer, because it weren't much work to get to that spot.

"I don't want to do that to someone else. Get 'em all hopped up like that. It's best people don't know."

I sat there about to cast and wondered if I should ask. Decided it would bug me the rest of the day if I didn't.

"What about me? You're taking me to these spots. Aren't you worried about me?"

"Nah, you live too far away. Besides, you're not as good a fisherman as he was."

———◆———

Pools of water. That's what you look for on the Oxtongue River, if you want to catch speckled trout. Pools of water at the base of rapids. In bends of the river. Mid-channel sometimes, right next to white water, which is not where you would expect to find deep water and if you can find one of those holes you'll do all right on the Oxtongue.

Fly fishermen tend to like running water, luring trout out of pools with the right fly, the right action. They know the time of day when the fish will be feeding, perhaps already in the moving water, keeping stationary on gravel beds by moving their tails, ready to rise to the surface and strike at anything twitching across the surface of the water.

We are not fly-fishing so we work the pools of water. Cast spinners into the pools and try different retrieves bringing the lure back. Slow. Fast. Slow with jerk. Fast with jerk. Slow-jerk-jerk. Jerk-jerk-fast.

At the second pool we fish Frank hooks a nice speckle but the fish flips the lure just as it gets close to the canoe. Disappearing before we have a good look at it. A flash of shadow and hazy red dots and then it's gone. Looked like a good fish and we stay thirty minutes on that pool but never get another bite.

Move to the next. Work that pool for half an hour without a strike. Paddle down-river looking for more deep water.

———◆———

It is turning into a hot morning and we have taken off our jackets, put aside our thermoses. There are only cirrus clouds in the sky, wispy white strands almost too high to see. By early afternoon even those will likely be gone and we will be fishing under a cloudless sky.

Frank is starting to worry that we have missed our chance at catching speckles. It's getting too hot. They'll go into hiding until the evening. We may have to switch to bass.

Just then I get a strike. A solid whomp I feel in my hands and that ripples up my arms like an electric charge. I pull back on my rod and it bows like a scythe. Frank stops talking. Looks at me fumbling to turn the reel.

"Holy Jeepers," he whispers.

————◆————

You can fish for years just to have fifteen minutes like the fifteen minutes coming up for me. Think that was a fair deal.

Pound for pound, there may no better game fish than speckled trout. No speckle ever took a fishing lure out of curiosity, inadvertence or boredom. They attack. After the whomp in my arm I start reeling in line, struggling to make every turn of the reel until Frank yells at me to loosen the drag. I'm going to snap the line.

I make the adjustment but turn the wheel too far at first, so the line goes racing off my spool. So quickly it seems to spin in the air. Flying off the reel. That's what I was looking at.

"Holy Jeepers," Frank whispers again.

I tighten the drag, pull back, and there is one more magnificent bend to my rod. I start reeling in line, slowly this time, letting out more line then I take in — two rotations in, three rotations out — then I switch the ratio around and start bringing the trout to the canoe.

A few minutes later, perhaps sensing it is losing the fight, the trout jumps. A high-arcing, rolling jump, that ends with the fish splashing on the water full-length, a geyser

LESSON THREE
Good Plants and How to Use Them

Frank uses plants and trees every day. To build fires. Flavour food. Cure stomach pains. Here are his ten favourite plants and trees:

Cedar

Chaga mushroom

1. Cedar "A wonder tree," says Frank. Cedar makes the best kindling wood, the best house siding and the best tea. It was cedar tea that saved Jacques Cartier.

2. Wintergreen Made into a tea, it helps with back pains, joint pains, headaches and fever. Frank's "wonder plant."

3. Chaga mushroom Ground into a tea it helps with stomach pains and headaches. Improves the immune system.

4. Goldenthread gets rid of stomach pains and improves digestion.

5. Horsetail A "living fossil," the horsetail plant is the last living genus in the Equisetaceae family, which reproduces by spores, rather than seeds. It is a diuretic and used to treat ulcers and kidney ailments.

6. Maple Canada's tree for a reason. Best burning wood in the forest. If you're hunkering down for the winter, it's maple you want to have stacked next to the hearth.

7. Marigolds Every garden needs marigolds. Great flower for keeping away slugs and earwigs.

8. Moss Nature's compass. Moss always grows on the north side of a tree.

9. Spruce Makes the best gum for repairing canoes and tent seams

10. Balsam Take a balsam twig, make a cut in it with your pocketknife and put the twig in the water. The gum released from the knife cut will act as a propellant. The twig will take off like a boat. A tree that gives you a toy.

Horsetail

Wintergreen

of water erupting. A couple walking the Western Uplands Trail comes over to see what is happening.

It takes another five minutes before the fish is in the net. When it was ten feet from the canoe it started bending my rod like some drunken water-diviner. Made quick, slashing turns and rolls. That fish never tired or gave, never treaded water beside the canoe, almost knocked the net out of Frank's hands when he first tried to bring it in.

Then the trout was high in the air, twisting and throwing off water, the speckles on the belly so large and luminous they looked like they had been sprayed on by a child's glitter gun.

"What do you figure?" I ask.

"Three pounds. Three-and-a-half. That is one nice fish. See how it almost knocked the net outta my hand?"

"I did."

""Gotta love speckles."

"You really do, don't you?"

———◆———

We catch two more speckles out of that pool, one each, both about a pound, but then it cools and we move downriver. Fish under a bridge for twenty minutes without any luck. Go for our shore lunch.

I watch Frank prepare our shore lunch and because it is such a ritualized activity, each movement near choreographed, and because I have seen it so many times, I notice when something different happens. He walks into the forest. Comes back with what looks like a blackened potato.

"What do you have there?"

"Chaga."

"Chaga? What in the world is that?"

"It's a mushroom. Or a fungus I 'spose. Grows on the top of birch trees."

"You're going to use it on the fish?"

"No. I'm bringing it home with me. I grind it up and drink it."

"What does it do?"

"Lots of stuff. Jeepers. It helps your immune system. Helps your kidneys. Helps if you got stomach pains. Some people say it fights cancer."

"Do you believe that?"

"I don't not believe it. I've seen it help people."

"Chaga. I'll have to look that up."

"Look it up? Hell, I'll make you a cup."

———◆———

One thing leads to another and before long we are talking about other plants Frank uses.

"Cedar may be my favourite," he says. "So many things you can do with cedar."

The conversation continues when we go back fishing. Talking about plants that are good for you. Frank saying that would be a good thing to record. Before long — and fishing conversations are well known for starting one place and migrating someplace so different you'd think everyone got lost along the way— we are talking about Jacques Cartier.

How Cartier had his life saved one winter when Mi'kmaq Indians came aboard his ice-locked ship and brewed him tea they made from a local plant, leading quickly to his recovery from scurvy. Cartier never recorded what the plant was and people guessed about its identity for the next four centuries.

"Stupid of him not to have drawn a picture or something," says Frank.

"Champlain wouldn't have made that mistake."

"You don't think?"

"Pretty sure. Champlain drew everything. Cartier hated to leave his ship. He was like a cruise ship passenger or something."

A shore lunch

We start debating Champlain versus Cartier. Fishing the Oxtongue River. Looking for deep pools of water. A cairn to Tom Thomson next lake over. I'm not sure if you could have a more Canadian moment. Maybe we needed a loon.

———◆———

Frank read in a museum in Pembroke that historians always wondered what sort of tea the Mi'kmaq made and after four centuries had concluded it must have been anneda tea, made from white cedar.

Which Frank would have told any historian if one had bothered to ask him. Cedar is a wonder tree, and cedar tea is well known for bringing down fevers. He couldn't understand debating a thing like that for four centuries.

The Mi'kmaq saved Cartier's life and he repaid them by kidnapping ten of them and taking them to France. There they were presented to King Francis I as either pets or zoo specimens — accounts differ — although it was much to the delight of the king, who rewarded Cartier with another commission, but after a few days grew bored with the Mi'kmaq and consigned them to one of his country estates, where they all contracted yellow fever and died within a few years.

I have just told Frank the Mi'kmaq story.

"It's hard to like that guy."

"Yep."

———◆———

Just before we are to head ashore and start portaging our way back to the Tea Lake Dam, we find another pool of water with speckle trout hiding. I catch two, one too small to keep, but the other a little over a pound. Frank catches one the same size.

With those two, plus the beautiful three-pounder I caught earlier in the day, there is a heft to my bag when I put it on my back and start walking toward the dam. It is a nice feeling, walking out of a lake or river in Algonquin Park with trout on your back.

When we are back in Whitney, Frank will fillet the trout on his table and wrap them in brown butcher's paper, present them to me as though presents. After that I will put them in my cooler and the next day I will drive home.

Sunday afternoon I will pull into my driveway and take out the cooler. That night I will barbecue the speckle trout and feed my family. Feel like a righteous provider for the rest of the evening.

Which makes no sense, because Monday morning I will do the same thing. I will go to work, where I will write for the Sun, do a radio show for Bellmedia — in effect write and talk — and then the writing and talking will be converted into money. That I will use to buy groceries.

Many times, when I eat trout brought back from Algonquin Park, I wonder why I complicate my life.

———◆———

There was not much left to burn. Some outbuildings by the shore. The dock. As for the grand inn itself, they were down to the foundation. They would dig that out as best they could, and start planting red pine later that week.

Frank stared at what was left of the Highland Inn, and as had happened for several days now, a wave of sadness came over him. The people who ran Algonquin Park didn't want the inn anymore, a decision he couldn't understand.

He had thought of taking mementos with him: some cutlery he could give to his mother; maybe some of the playing cards with the Grand Trunk Railway logo on it, for his dad. But someone had been fired two weeks ago for trying to leave with a Wedgwood teacup, so he had decided against it.

The Highland Inn

When they burned off the wood the bonfire was large enough to be seen at the Western Gates of the Park. Huge plumes of smoke drifted over the hills for many days. When the smoke was gone, so was the inn.

He couldn't understand why anyone would want to get rid of something as grand as the Highland Inn. Same as he couldn't understand wanting to get rid of the train, which some people said was going to happen soon.

All the Sports came by train. How would they come now?

He was only twenty-three but didn't like how things were changing in the Park. Too much change, coming too fast. With the Highland Inn now closed all of the inns and lodges that still hired guides were outside the Park.

Which was beyond strange.

He picked up his shovel and looked again at the foundation. He doubted if they could remove the stairs. Give it a try, he guessed.

As he walked toward the foundation it occurred to him that he had ended up working at the Highland Inn. Pretty much the last one to do so.

LESSON FOUR
How to Belong Somewhere

"You askin' me what I like about Algonquin Park is not as easy to answer as you might think.

"I like fishin' in the Park but there's good fishin' lots of places. I like trees and that must be part of it. I can name all the trees 'round here and we've got 'em all. Some days I like just walkin' through the woods, checkin' out what the trees are doing.

"I like lakes almost as much as I like trees. ...(I would) feel all mixed up if I had to live on the prairies, or by an ocean. I don't like wide-open horizons. I like things in front of me.

"(And then) there's the animals. I haven't spoken 'bout them yet but that would be part of it. I still get a rush when I see a bull moose standing in the reeds, or hear a wolf in the middle of the night.

"Anytime that happens I try to picture where the wolf is; what it might be doin' right then. If I lived anywhere else I don't think I could do that — hear an animal and 'magine what it was doing.

"(I can) close my eyes anytime I want and 'magine what different animals might be doing in Algonquin Park. What different people might be doin' and the way different places would look right then.

"Knowin' a place so well you can do a thing like that is when you know you're livin' where you belong. If you can't do a thing like that, you should probably move."

THE
LAST GUIDE'S
GUIDE

Year Two

Earth's the right place for love:
I don't know where it's likely to go better.

— Robert Frost, "Birches"

I have learned that to be with those I like is enough.

— Walt Whitman, "I Sing the Body Electric"

◆4◆

Signs of spring — Opening Day — The difference between good and bad — A pet crow — The missing-sheets incident — Fishing Costello Lake

The winter of 2012-13 was a mild one for most of Canada. The exception was the Prairies, which for the second year running had snow on the ground by Thanksgiving that stayed until Easter.

Everywhere else there was flooding. In Ontario, cottages in the Muskokas and Georgian Bay area were swept away not in April but in February. The Calgary Flood that nearly shut down the Stampede was that year. Toronto was flooded. Much of Atlantic Canada was flooded.

In Ottawa the traditional one-week January thaw lasted most of the month. The weather was so mild there were concerns that events at the capital's annual winter festival — Winterlude — would need to be cancelled. If not the entire festival.

But February kicked in good and strong, the festival was saved, and winter ran from then until Saint Patrick's Day. It was pretty much gone after that, although there was one freakish storm the first week of April.

Despite the mild season, there was still a waiting-for-winter-to-end air in the nation's capital that March, as most people in Ottawa believe winter is twice as long as necessary to begin with.

People began the annual search for signs of spring. For dirt being sold in plastic bags at a big-box grocery somewhere. A crocus appearing on Parliament Hill. Perhaps a federal politician walking around town with a travel brochure sticking out from a blazer pocket (parliamentarians traditionally begin summer holidays a month before most grade-school students.)

In the Algonquin Highlands people were doing the same. They looked for moose by the side of Highway 60, the animals lured down from the hills by salt pushed to the side of the road during winter. The moose stood there licking the salt and paying no attention whatsoever to the cars that came screeching to a halt when they were spotted.

Or painting crews working at one of the motels in town, spring being the time of year for such work. Perhaps a bag of ice being sold at the Freshmart grocery. Which stocks ice all year round. Although in winter it is mostly for conversation.

———◆———

The surest sign of spring arriving in the Algonquin Highlands will not come by way of a moose sighting, painting crews or the sale of bagged ice. In the spring of 2013 the sign came the day Frank drove to Arowhon Pines Resort to inspect a large, dead pine the resort wanted removed.

Frank did not bother to get out of his van when he got there, seeing the tree the other side of Little Joe Lake and knowing there was no way he was bringing it across a frozen lake as he would have liked. Little Joe was already open.

Even the creek running in from Canoe Lake was open and although at first Frank thought he saw what looked like chips of ice flowing out the mouth of the creek, when he pulled out his field glasses he saw it wasn't even that. The creek was running so high it had white caps.

After that he went to bring in an ice-fishing hut he had taken off Lake of Bays the previous week, finding the hut good and dry, no ice or snow on it and Lake of Bays open as far as he could see. He took the hut home and placed it next to two other huts he had already brought in.

Then he loaded his van with two cords of split maple and drove to Paradise Road, where he had winter customers. He dropped off two half-cords and found his third customer standing in her front yard, throwing corn kernels to her hens, a rooster and a handful of ducks that had wandered into the yard.

"Afternoon Frank."

"Afternoon Ethel."

"With this weather I don't know if I'll need a full cord."

"You probably won't. Why don't I leave half a- cord and you can call me if you need more."

"That's what I'll do, Frank," and she reached into the pocket of her apron, took out some folded bills and passed them to him.

"Whyda feed the ducks?" he asked, putting the money in his pocket.

"I've got the corn."

Frank nodded, thinking that was a good answer.

He gassed up his van, went to the post office to get his mail and was home cooking supper shortly after five. That night, after he had cleared the dishes and made a cup of coffee, Frank turned on his television and sat at his kitchen table, watching fishermen going after bonefish off the coast of Cuba. He had heard many stories about bonefish. Some considered the fish one of the best game fish going, on a par with speckles, and he watched the show with interest.

In a few minutes though, as always happened when Frank watched television shows about people fishing in the Caribbean — not a tree anywhere — he got bored and turned away. In a few minutes he reached across the table

Frank on the verandah of Arowhon Pines Resort

to grab a laminated map from a stack of maps, papers and magazines that always sat on the edge of his table.

Didn't really need the map. But it was tradition. To pull out this map when it was time to start getting ready for Opening Day.

Frank took a sip of coffee and started placing his finger on various blotches of blue, working his way across *The Canoe Routes of Algonquin Park*.

———◆———

While Frank was looking at his map I was looking at last year's interviews, anxious to return to the Algonquin Highlands and continue working on the guidebook. I had the first few chapters written, as well as half a dozen lessons.

I had spent much of the winter thinking about our two fishing trips and when I looked at the transcribed interviews I thought something was starting to emerge. Frank's world-view, if not clearly visible yet, had been sighted. The major tenets anyway.

What made Frank so happy and contented had something to do with belonging someplace. Not being afraid of competition or adventure. Being outside more than inside.

I figured one or two more fishing trips and I'd have it all worked out.

———◆———

Because of the mild winter, come Opening Day of trout season every lake in Algonquin Park was open, not much snow left even on the portage trails. Lakes that in many years you couldn't reach until mid-May, or later, could be reached that year. Frank had spent weeks looking at his map, enjoying the possibilities.

His first client of the year was Jack Mihell, a retired conservation officer from Barry's Bay who had booked Frank for Opening Day of trout season for the past twenty-two years. The other day Frank heard someone say on the country music station out of Bancroft that there used to be good guitar players in this world, great guitar players, and Chet Atkins.

You could say a similar thing about Jack Mihell. There are sport fishermen in this world, serious sport fishermen, and Jack Mihell.

Mihell spent summer holidays with his wife fishing out of sea kayaks on Georgian Bay. Helped stock every stocked lake in Algonquin Park. Had never missed Opening Day of trout season since he was a young man first posted to Barry's Bay. Now that he was retired and living in Sudbury, he still came to Whitney the last Saturday of each April, driving down on the Friday and driving back to Sudbury come Sunday.

The year before, when he was waiting for eye surgery, Frank had never called Mihell to tell him he might not be able to guide him that Opening Day. He phoned me. He phoned every other client.

But he couldn't phone Jack Mihell. Figuring there were some things in this world that were good for people to know, and some things that were bad, and telling Jack Mihell his fishing guide might be in the hospital on Opening Day struck him as one of the bad ones.

When Mihell arrived at his front door that year he looked at Frank's eye-patch and said:

"You can still fish, right?"

"I can still fish."

"Good. Where should I put my gear?"

It was only some time later, when the gear was safely stowed away and Mihell was sitting at Frank's kitchen table drinking coffee that he got around to asking:

"What's with the eye?"

"I can't see out it."

"You need surgery?"

"Yep."

"That'll take care of it?"

"Maybe. 'Cording to some twelve-year-old doctor."

"Just the one eye."

"So far."

"Any pain?"

"Not since I got some liniment to put on it. Prescription stuff."

"You're not in any pain now."

"No."

"Well, you look like a Polish pirate. Where are we going fishing?"

The next day Mihell took a pocket GPS with him in case Frank's bum eye caused "orienteering problems" although it was mostly to show off the new GPS, which Mihell said could pinpoint his location to within a metre anywhere in North America. He turned on the machine the night he arrived and showed Frank how it worked, but Frank said he wasn't sure how impressed he should be because it was pretty clear Jack was standing in his kitchen.

The GPS fell in the lake shortly after they started fishing the next morning and they walked out that afternoon with eight brook trout, the biggest nearly four pounds and none less than two. One of the best Opening Days in a decade.

———◆———

Mihell is already there when I arrive. He and Frank are sitting at the kitchen table, watching the fishing channel with the volume turned down.

"So you think they have that channel salted with fish, Frank?" asks Mihell, after I sit at the table with them. He is pointing at the television, where a young man is holding aloft what looks to be a pike well in excess of ten pounds.

"Sure of it," says Frank. "They been getting strikes every time they pass that camera they have set up by the channel.

Ain't no one that talented."

"How do they do it?"

"Nets. They have 'em netted off in back of the channel. Probably using jacklights as well, to bring 'em to the surface."

We watch as another pike is hooked and brought to the boat.

"Still a nice fish," says Frank. "Just a shame they're fishing in an aquarium."

———◆———

After we have supper — venison stew, twelve-grain bread and butter-tarts for desert — I take out some of the transcribed interviews and start going through them with Frank. I show him some of the lessons. He asks how many lessons I was planning on having and I say I'm not sure.

"How about twelve?" he says. Frank is an old twelve-steps guy. The suggestion doesn't surprise me.

"That might work," I say.

"You've got the fishing lures right," says Mihell, giving Frank an approving nod. "What else are you going to have in there?"

Frank considers the question. What would make sense to talk about, after you've already talked about fishing lures, the Algonquin Highlands and Chaga mushrooms?

"Good things and bad things," he says finally. "How to tell the difference 'tween them. That would be a good thing for people to know."

———◆———

Later that night, in a first attempt at explaining the difference between good things and bad things, Frank tells a story about Basil Sawyer, Walter's father.

Sawyer was working as a guide at the Highland Inn, taking a client lake trout fishing one day, a rich client who owned a gold smelting company in Fort Erie. Bud Williams

Basil Sawyer with lake trout caught on Opeongo Lake

was an avid lake trout fisherman who dreamed of catching trophy fish, of seeing his name in *Field and Stream* one day. He had begun smelting his own trolling lures, in the hopes this would give him a competitive edge.

One day, Williams was fishing with Basil Sawyer, using one of his homemade lures, which looked a little like the stem of a soup spoon, and although he had caught a few respectable lakers it was nothing to write home about and certainly nothing that was ever going to get him into *Field and Stream.*

Near the end of the day Sawyer asked if he could see the lure. He held it in his hand and examined it. Ran his fingers along the edge and held it up to the sun. Closed one eye and looked at the lure sideways, lengthwise, then cupped it in the palm of his hand and skimmed it through the water.

After he had done all that Sawyer took a pair of pliers from the breast pocket of his blazer, a jacket some Sport had given him, applied the pincers to the middle of the lure and twisted.

He gave the bent lure back to Williams.

"Try that."

"Try what? You've just ruined it, Basil."

Sawyer didn't say anything.

"It's twisted all out of shape," continued Williams. "It's just a hunk of metal now. This thing is going to go through the water like an anchor."

By this time Sawyer had resumed paddling and merely shrugged his shoulders. It was up to the Sport.

After another moment of silence, Williams wondering if he should complain about Sawyer when they got back to the Highland Inn (not an easy call to make as Sawyer had been a good guide up until then), the businessman snorted and tossed the lure into the water. Removed the catch on his reel. If he was going to complain, he better make sure Sawyer saw for himself what a mess he had made.

Legend has it a lake trout struck that lure before Williams finished letting out his line, a fish that would be recorded by *Field and Stream* that winter as the largest lake trout caught in North America. Right out of Lake of Two Rivers. On Sawyer's mangled lure.

When he returned to Fort Erie Williams had his smelters make scores of the new lure and gave them away at the Highland Inn next season to anyone who asked for one. That winter the Williams Gold Smelting Company was inundated with requests from fishermen across North America who had heard of the lure and wanted to purchase one.

Within a few years there was no more smelting company. In its place stood the Williams Fishing Lure Company, still operating today, a company that built its success on the lure Basil Sawyer reportedly fashioned in a canoe one day, using a pair of pliers: the Williams Wabler.

Legend further has it Williams asked Sawyer years later what gave him the idea of bending the lure. Sawyer reportedly answered:

"Your lure was straight. Ain't nothing in this world ever straight. Fish would know that."

———◆———

"Fish would know that," says Frank one more time, laughing harder then he did the first time. "Man, Basil was a good guide. Shame about his son."

"How does that help us pick out good things from bad, though?" I ask, thinking Frank must have forgotten the start of our conversation. "You can't go around all the time asking what a fish would think of something."

"No you can't," he agrees. "Wish you could, but you can't. So you ask the next question."

"Which is?"

"Do it look natural to you?"

Frank, standing still for a moment

———◆———

While Frank and Jack were gone on Opening Day, I borrowed a canoe and went to Brewer Lake. It's right off Highway 60 almost as soon as you enter Algonquin Park from the eastern gate. No portaging required. Without Frank as my guide I am never as serious about fishing as I should be and it was mid-morning (if you are charitable and define 11:00 as mid-morning) before I had the canoe in the water.

I paddled to some cliffs on the eastern shore of the lake and began fishing. Casting a Black Fury spinner toward the cliffs and bringing it back. After half an hour without any luck I changed the spinner to a hook and worm, attached a bobber, cast to within five feet of the cliffs and let the worm sit there.

I sat back in the canoe and looked around. Not sure if I even wanted to catch a fish right then. If I fell asleep and started drifting that would be fine.

I thought about the Williams Wabler story. It showed how Frank determines good from bad. What made the lure good wasn't that it was natural. A lot of people make that mistake: assuming that if something is natural, it's good for you. Don't need anything more than that. End of story.

But Frank wasn't saying that. What made the lure good was that it worked. It caught a lake trout. Being natural was a trait of many good things, but not the defining thing. Good and bad are determined by utility.

Which might sound pretty obvious and simple until you start putting together a list of all the things people think are good for them but probably aren't — high-carb diets, hockey summer camps, translated cookbooks, on-line newspapers, political pundits, polling companies, credit cards, deficit financing, and most forms of government could be on the list.

People have convinced themselves these things work for reasons that have nothing to do with utility. They are good because: My son may play in the NHL. I'm fat. That guy is smarter than me. I need this car. This form of government is better than the alternative.

It gets even more complicated when you consider how many things in this world are demonstrably bad for you — flat-out bad ideas — people go ahead and do anyway: smoking, eating cheeseburgers, building nuclear weapons, breaching parole, marrying Angelina Jolie, jogging past the age of fifty.

Most of us determine what is good and what is bad by using a complex system of trade-offs, rationalizations, ideologies, politics, aspirations and delusions. Frank doesn't. With an empiricism a scientist would envy, he looks at something and decides if it's working. Then decides if it's good or bad.

He has no follow-up questions.

———◆———

When I get back to Frank's, he is standing at the fillet table, working on the speckle trout he and Jack have caught. Six beautiful speckles, none looking smaller than two pounds. I hand over the one small splake I have managed to catch on Brewer Lake and go sit with Mihell.

As Frank works a crow watches him from a light post across the road. The crow is normally there when Frank is working at the fillet table. One of the biggest crows I have ever seen. When it flies overhead, if the bird is low enough and passes directly over you, its wingspan will cast you in shadows.

When he's finished with half the fish, Frank takes a bucket of guts, walks to the end of the driveway and throws it on the gravel. The crow is in the air before Frank has turned around.

I look at the crow marching beside my car, tossing its head and swallowing the fish guts. The animal had the strut of a parade grand marshal. If you could have placed a tiny baton in its talons the effect would have been complete.

During past visits I have seen Frank click his teeth to summon the crow. Have seen him stand in the driveway and watch the bird eat, in no hurry to walk away with the guts bucket, standing so close he could have reached down and petted it.

"You know that crow is practically a pet," I say.

"Ain't no pet."

"Are you sure? You call it. You feed it. If that bird had four feet it would be a dog."

Frank finishes filleting the rest of the fish, looking annoyed while he works, then he walks down his driveway and throws away the last of the guts. When the bird starts eating and strutting I imagine a John De Souza march playing in the background.

"Too useful to be a pet," he says, when he's sitting beside us. He watches as the bird tears into the fish guts, getting rid of what would have been a bag of garbage Frank would have needed to take to the roadside come Tuesday.

"Maybe its livestock," he says, "Useful enough to be livestock. But it ain't no pet."

———◆———

That night I realized Frank wasn't annoyed with me because I had called the crow a pet, and that would be odd: having a crow as a pet. He was annoyed because I was forgetting the Golden Rule of utility.

Why would he have a pet? He doesn't need a dog to go for a walk. Doesn't need a cat for companionship.

There was nothing wrong with other people owning pets, but Frank had no need. So I was accusing him not of being odd, but of being frivolous. I was probably insulting the crow too.

It's not hard to get Frank annoyed. Comically easy, really. Get a lure snagged. Cast upriver. Throw away something that can be reused or recycled. Ever since the *Toronto Star* called *The Last Guide*, "a homage to a vanishing way of life," you can use the word "homage" around him with great results.

He is a man of strong opinions. Earned honestly. Knowing that very little is knee-jerk or un-considered about Frank, I have learned to respect them, even if I don't agree.

I don't tease Frank about the crow anymore. Still like teasing him about the *Toronto Star.*

———◆———

The next morning Frank and I go fishing on Costello Lake, right off the access road to Opeongo Lake. It is a lake thousands of anglers pass each summer on their way to Opeongo, not giving it much thought. A fished-out lake. If you were going to stop at all at Costello — and this might be the telltale sign of any fished-out lake — it would be to use the nearby picnic grounds.

Frank normally catches his limit of splake on Costello Lake. Has good luck with speckles in the spring and fall. He will often come to Costello Lake on a Sunday, a day he normally doesn't work, although he makes exceptions for the beginning and end of trout season.

We park the van in the parking lot for the picnic grounds and carry the canoe over to the lake. Put it in by a culvert, and then start trolling down the east shore. We have casting rods with us as well, in case we want to try for speckles later in the day.

———◆———

Although I have been in Whitney for a day, it doesn't feel like I've arrived until I am in the canoe fishing with Frank. We even start talking as though I have just arrived.

LESSON FIVE
How to Talk to Customer Service People

"I bought an electric fish-fillet knife once and burn'd the motor out in less than a month. Bought it at the Stedman's store in Barry's Bay, and they gave me another one no problem.

"That one lasted two weeks.

"I took the knife apart to see what the problem was and it was real easy to spot. The company had started using a plastic gear, where there used to be a brass one.

"I contacted the company. Figured they should know what was happening.

"(I got) this customer-service woman on the phone and explained what was happening.

"She thanked me for phoning. She was polite and all. She wasn't the first customer service person I spoke to, people kept transferring me, 'til I got to her, so I maybe got the politest person down there.

"After I was finished, she told me I wasn't using the knife properly.

"Not using the knife properly?"

"That's right Mr. Kuiack. Think about it along with me for a minute. Can we do that? I've never taken a call from someone who says the motor of the knife has burned out. You say this has happened to you twice?"

"That's right,"

"Shouldn't that give you something to think about?"

"I guess it does."

"You can see what I'm saying."

"I suppose. Though I don't see why I should get punished just 'cuz I'm the first good fisherman that's ever called ya."

"Eugene passed away. I guess you heard that," says Frank.

He is talking about Eugene Kates, the man who owned Arowhon Pines Resort, along with his wife, Helen, where Frank has been guiding for several years.

"I did. He was a great guy. How old was he?"

"Made it to ninety-four."

"Good life."

"Yep. Sure was. Helen is still there."

"I saw her last year."

"Her health isn't good. Theresa is pretty much running the place now."

"She's always sort of run the place."

"Right on."

"Did you know Eugene's mom?"

"Never met her. My brother Dominique worked for her. Said the only way you could win an argument with her was if you picked her up and threw her into the lake."

"He actually did that?"

"More than once."

"That's funny. Did Eugene ever tell you the missing sheets story?"

"Couple times. He loved that story."

"He loved his mom."

"Right on."

———◆———

Arowhon Pines Resort, one of the finest resorts in the Algonquin Highlands, was founded in 1938 by Lillian Kates, a woman of tremendous internal strength and resolve, like an ironwood sapling some said, although others were of the opinion any tough, unyielding object — fire poker, leather sap — would make an apt analogy.

Although not from the Algonquin Highlands, Kates was quick to adopt the ways and manners of those who lived

The view of Little Joe Lake, from the verandah
at Arowhon Pines Resort

here. Or perhaps she arrived with the attitude. It seemed natural enough.

Although she was a fastidious innkeeper, Kates expected her guests to behave. Actions that could be construed as misbehaving were many and varied. Not turning over a canoe when returning from a fishing trip was misbehaving. Not using the spittoons on the verandah. Being born German.

Guests that misbehaved were soon seated at a dining table next to the swinging kitchen doors. Given cold towels when returning from a swim, not the steamed towels other guests received. Were asked, whenever Kates saw them on the grounds, when they were leaving.

In extreme cases — these being misbehaving guests who returned a second time — she would make them wait in the lobby for hours before checking in. Made sure plates of food were paraded past them at meal times, Kates explaining she would love to offer them something to eat, but they hadn't checked into a room yet.

As far as anyone can recall there was only one misbehaving guest that came back a third time. An insurance adjustor from Kitchener, Ontario who had made the mistake one day of stepping on some basil plants Kates was growing near the back door of the kitchen. The guest apologized profusely for what he had done. But the basil plants were still dead.

The night after the basil killing the man was seated in the dining room next to the swinging doors. He didn't seem to mind. Even seemed to enjoy watching the food as it was being brought out.

He never noticed the cold towels. When Kates asked when he was leaving he was touched that the innkeeper cared so much about him.

Not having encountered such resistance before, Kates

became more creative in trying to push the man down the road. She told him he shouldn't go swimming anymore because there was a parasite in Little Joe Lake attracted to portly white men from Southern Ontario.

He thanked her for the warning.

She told him he couldn't sit on the verandah chewing tobacco and using her spittoons as the brand of tobacco he used turned the spittoons green. When the man pointed out that all the spittoons were green, Kates said she had no idea he chewed that much tobacco.

He promised to bring a different brand of tobacco next year.

There seemed no way of getting rid of him. Until Kates realized one day he was always one of the last guests to arrive in the dining room after the breakfast bell had been rung. Never fished early in the morning. Never really saw him much before nine a.m.

That man liked to sleep.

———◆———

When the man arrived the next summer, Kates was waiting for him.

First she inspected the pouches of chewing tobacco he had brought. Four different brands. When she was done, she told him they would all turn her spittoons green.

If he needed to chew he would need to go into the woods. A far ways too, as she wasn't at all sure what his tobacco was doing to her plants. He must remember the basil incident.

"Not a problem," said the man. "I chew mostly when I go fishing."

He then sat down, opened his travel satchel and took out a book and a mason jar of sauerkraut. He was preparing for the long wait to check into his room. The man opened his book, then the mason jar, slid a handful of sauerkraut into his mouth (he no longer asked for cutlery as his sauerkraut tarnished the silverware) and made himself comfortable.

When he had done all that, Kates leaned over the reception desk, and in almost a whisper said:

"Your room is ready."

"What. Ready now?" the man said, almost choking on his cabbage.

"Yes. But I should warn you. There is a problem with your bed."

"What sort of problem?"

"It's a new bed and we don't have sheets that fit."

"Well, no problem. I can use a sleeping bag I suppose."

"Those don't fit either."

The man stood there not knowing what to say. Did sleeping bags need to fit anything? Wasn't that rather the point of sleeping bags? Zip them up and there's your bed?

He asked if he might try a sleeping bag but Kates said she was sure it would ruin the new bed. So no.

When the man got to his room, sure enough, there were no sheets on his bed. It didn't look any different from last year's bed, but he was an insurance adjuster, not an engineer or bed-maker, so maybe there was a difference he didn't notice.

There were no pillows either and when he asked Kates about that during dinner she said the pillows didn't match the sheets. When the man pointed out there were no sheets, she said he should be able see the problem then.

The next morning the businessman was still one of the last guests to arrive for breakfast, but he yawned mightily over his bacon, rubbed his eyes while eating desert, and when he went fishing the guide said he fell asleep in the canoe.

The next morning the man was in the dining room just a

few minutes after the breakfast bell. The third morning he
was on the verandah waiting. The fourth morning he left.

When he was checking out, the man asked when the
new sheets might be arriving and Kates said she wasn't
sure. There had been some sort of problem at the bed-sheet
factory.

"Will you be getting rid of the new beds then?" he asked
and Kates looked at him with surprise.

"Why would I do that? It's a perfectly good bed."

———◆———

We start catching splake by the culvert. Four of them in
less than an hour, nothing big and they don't put up much
of a fight, but we put them on a stringer for Frank to fillet
later that afternoon.

We move away from the culvert and troll down the middle of Costello, looking for lakers, but don't find any. Frank
thinks he has a school on his fish finder for a while and we
chase that, but if it's lakers they're not biting.

We paddle down to Costello Creek, which connects up to
Brewer Lake, and take out our casting rods. Try for speckles. We work a few pools that look promising but have no
luck there, either.

Shortly before noon Frank asks if I want to go back to
the culvert.

"We can probably get some more splake," he says.

"I'm good. I came up here mostly to go through the guidebook with you. There's enough on the stringer for supper.
Why don't we head back?"

———◆———

Frank fillets two of the splake for me, wraps them in butcher's paper and I put them in the cooler in the back of my
jeep.

"When are you coming back up?" he asks.

"Family fishing day."

"That's right. I forgot. You going to bring your son?"

"Yes. He's looking forward to seeing you again."

"Tell 'em he's got to catch fish this time."

"I will."

"He needs to practice his action."

"I'll tell him, Frank."

"If you're teaching him he'll need some help. Tell 'em I'll be waiting."

◆ 5 ◆

Family Fishing Day — Frank and Marie — Meeting the ambassador of Rock Lake — The run-a-ways

The day before we leave for Algonquin Park, my son and I go to a Canadian Tire store to purchase supplies. We will be camping for this trip and it is a Corbett tradition, going to a Canadian Tire store before heading up to Algonquin Park. My own father was incapable of doing one without the other, returning each spring to the camping aisle of Canadian Tire like some migrating bird.

There, he would purchase Red Devil lures and Coleman fuel; foam coolers that always managed to fall apart before we returned to Ottawa. (All of my childhood camping memories end with me helping my father bail water out the trunk of some big old Ford, my father complaining under his breath about the shoddy workmanship being done these days at foam-cooler factories.)

I don't purchase a foam cooler but buy the Red Devil lures and the camping fuel (propane for my generation.) Also a pocketknife for William, who is nine now and that's about the age when I got my first pocketknife.

It is a good one, on sale that day, and when I give it to him I repeat the advice my father gave me.

"Never run with the blade open. Do you understand?"

"Yes."

"Only open the blade when you have something to do. A knife is a tool. Only use it when there's a job to be done."

"All right"

"Never throw a knife."

"All right."

"Promise?"

"Promise."

And off he runs. I know the work requiring use of a pocketknife will be quite inventive for the next few days. I am just hoping he doesn't start any jobs in the Canadian Tire store.

We go to a grocery next, where I find myself thinking if this were truly a shopping trip from my father's day, the steak I am buying would be minute and the milk would be powdered. As I go through the store putting items in the cart I begin to feel guilty about buying fresh fruit and granola bars, farm-fresh sour cream, something called "Camp-Sized" marshmallows that, when William comes running up to show me, I don't believe are real..

"That's one marshmallow? You're sure it's not stuck together somehow?"

To alleviate this guilt (and it was happening with greater frequency I had noticed, making consumer purchases that left me not feeling glad and responsible but anxious, nervous and momentarily wondering if I had lost my mind) I go in search of powdered milk.

Can't find it. Apparently they don't sell it anymore.

———◆———

We leave the next morning, after I have filed two columns for the Ottawa Sun, finished last-edits on a magazine feature, booked time off from the radio show and after all that have bought myself five days without deadlines.

We throw in the pop-up tent we are going to use for the trip, even though it has a busted zipper, because William likes the pop-up feature and you can block the hole in the zipper with a sleeping bag easily enough. Put the cooler next to the tent. Two sleeping bags. Fishing rods and tackle boxes.

We don't have to bother with a canoe. William knows how that works and has already asked me what sort of boat Frank will have for us this year.

"I have no idea."

"The last one had dents in it."

"I know."

"Big dents."

"I know."

It was true. We had fished from an aluminum boat he had pulled from the bottom of Cache Lake. A large dent on the port side he had never been able to hammer out properly. A boxer's-nose dent to the bow.

"Don't worry," I say. "The boat will be fine."

———◆———

We get out of Ottawa at a decent time and as soon as I make the turn from the Trans-Canada Highway to Highway 60, I ease up on the gas pedal. There had been hundreds of things to do but now we are on the road.

We drive through Eganville and then Wilno. In Barry's Bay we stop for an early lunch and walk around the town afterwards. I show William the garage where my dad's cars ended up a lot of summers, one car never making it out of the garage, dying right there on the hoist. That summer we had to rent a cottage on Aylen Lake instead of camping in Algonquin Park.

Because the car was dead and Aylen Lake was only a few miles away. That was a good summer.

———◆———

We drive right through Whitney, which seems strange, so accustomed have I become to making the turn to Frank's home. A few minutes later we are in the Park and a few moments after that, making the turn into the Rock Lake Campgrounds.

I had made the reservation on-line months ago and was not disappointed when we got to our campsite. A large site with mature hardwood trees for shade and hanging rope lines, a view of Rock Lake, not far from the beach, another campsite behind us to the right but none on the other sides.

"Sweet," says William, already taking the pop-up tent out of the car.

We pop the tent, throw in our packs and sleeping bags, buy firewood at a depot not far away, put the wood under a tarp along with our cook stove and ax and an hour later we are on our way to Frank's.

——◆——

He has a full house when we arrive. For the first time in the thirteen years I have been coming to visit Frank he is not the one to answer the door. Or shout out his sunroom window: "Come'n up, door's open."

It is an attractive woman in her late '30s, a granddaughter of Frank's I will soon learn, visiting from Guelph. She's going through a nasty divorce and wanted to get out of town for a few days, and so yesterday she decided to drive all day and part of the night so she could get to her grandfather's house and go fishing.

"Think it did her some good," says Frank, when we are sitting in his sunroom a few minutes later. "Took her out for small-mouth. Caught twenty-three of them."

The granddaughter from Guelph is not the only surprise in the house this day. In a few minutes I hear a baby cry. I look at Frank and he shrugs.

"Bunch of people here for the fishing derby," he says. A few minutes later another woman I have never met comes into the sunroom. Younger than the granddaughter from Guelph. She is cradling a baby.

"This is Summers. She's up from Guelph for the derby as well."

I shake the one free hand the young woman offers me and I say:

"So you're another of Frank's granddaughters, Summers?"

They both laugh and it is Frank who answers.

"Summers is my great-granddaughter, Ron."

I don't say anything right away. Although I notice William is doing the same thing I have started doing. Staring at the baby.

The week before I had done a story about the Battle of Crysler Farm, the only battle in the War of 1812 to take place in Eastern Ontario. A woman I interviewed was a descendent of one of the heroes of that battle. And if my math was right, the family relationship between that woman and her famous ancestor was the same relationship as the one between Frank and that baby.

I ask just to confirm.

"The baby's name is ..."

"Liam," says Frank.

"And Liam is ..."

"My great-great grandson."

———◆———

Frank noticed her the moment she walked on the bus. Carrying a duffel bag that might have been bigger than her.

The bus was on its way to Timmins, where Frank had been living the past two years. He was working in the mines, half-a-mile underground, where the sun was something you were going to see at the end of your workday and not a minute before.

He hated it.

He had left Whitney because he couldn't find steady work but he came back as often as possible. Was coming back right then from a fishing trip where he had caught a four-pound speckle on Source Lake, a fish so beautiful last night he dreamed about it.

He took another look at her. She was sitting two rows up, in the aisle seat, so Frank could see the side of her face. She had black curly hair and eyes that darted around the bus, never resting long on any object, never staring.

She's taking it all in, thought Frank. She wants to make sure she knows where she's sitting. Down to every last detail. Doesn't want any surprises.

It was what he had done six hours ago, when he had boarded the bus in Huntsville.

He didn't know at the time why she would be so wary. Did not know she had been widowed twice, was raising eleven children and living further from home than he was.

Just knew she had eyes that didn't rest. And maybe, just maybe, she was shorter than he was.

He stood up and walked to the aisle seat, two rows up.

————◆————

That night, at our campsite, we roast some of the camp-size marshmallows. They aren't bad. As we are roasting them it comes back to me that I would often shove two or three marshmallows onto a stick when I was a boy, because one never seemed proper reward for not burning the marshmallow or losing it in the campfire. Camp-sized marshmallows. I would have wanted these.

"Do you believe Frank has a great-great granddaughter?" William asks, his eyes carefully watching the marshmallow he is holding over the fire.

"Crazy isn't it?"

"I don't see how it's even possible."

"Big family. Lot of years. It won't happen all that often."

"How much family does Frank have?"

"Holy jeepers."

"Daaaaad."

Frank by the campfire

"All right. Sorry. My gosh William, he would have a lot. He had eighteen brothers and sisters. He had thirteen children himself."

"Thirteen?"

"Yep. He had two with his first wife, and then Marie had eleven children."

"So they're step-kids?"

"He lived with them. Helped raise them. I've never once heard him call them his stepchildren."

"It's still freaky. Thirteen children."

"I suppose."

"They all seem to like him."

"That's probably the freakiest part."

———◆———

Family Fishing Week in Ontario is traditionally held the first week of July. For this week, anyone in the province can fish without a licence. Children's fishing derbies are often held this week.

Some years ago ice fishermen in Ontario started complaining about "summer bias" and so the province added another week in February. While this was tolerant and inclusive on the part of the government, it rather destroyed the title of the event. How can you call it Family Fishing Week when there are two weeks?

To correct this linguistic problem the province now calls both weeks Family Fishing Events. Which keeps everyone happy, as the phrase is more or less meaningless.

Algonquin Park was an early promoter of Family Fishing Week and as ice fishing is banned in the Park, it remains Family Fishing Week.

Each year the Park organizes a child's fishing derby for the Saturday. It is normally held on Whitefish Lake and has grown in popularity through the years. When we arrive at Whitefish Lake the next morning there are so many cars arriving, conservation officers are directing traffic in the parking lot.

Down by the shore it's just as busy, with boats lined up to take children fishing. There is an Ontario Parks boat, with a massive hull and central console and it looks more like a Boston Whaler than a cottage fishing boat. There is a boat from the OPP water rescue team, so many gadgets and shining lights it looks like something you would find in an amusement park.

There are several boats from cottagers in the Park: A beautiful, wooden Adirondack skiff. A new Princecraft. What looks like a new Lund.

And then there is Frank's boat: a low-gunneled, Mirro Seaquest from the '80s, hand-painted a blue colour that keeps changing hue — from new denim to robin's egg — as it works its way around the hull.

There is a knot of children around Frank's boat waiting to go fishing; so large it is practically embarrassing for the other boaters.

Children know a pirate boat when they see one.

———◆———

I send William off fishing with Frank and stroll around the Whitefish Lake picnic grounds. The OPP are here for the fishing derby, helping man a Crime Prevention booth giving away red-devil lures and fridge magnets in the shape of trout. Emergency numbers for South Algonquin Township are printed underneath the fins.

Kevin Heinz is here as well, getting ready for the fish fry that will take place once the children have returned from fishing. He is not counting on the children providing the meal. He has 20,000 rock-bass fillets in coolers by his feet.

"How long did it take you to catch 20,000 rock bass?"

"An afternoon," says Heinz.

"One afternoon?"

Bailing out the Mirro Seaquest

"Part of a night too."

"Are you serious?"

"No."

Turns out it took close to two months, Heinz and Frank fishing Galeairy Lake every evening. With triple hooks and buckets of worms. Pulling up six fish at a time.

I keep walking around the picnic grounds and in a minute a man comes up and introduces himself as the ambassador of Rock Lake.

"You're a friend of Frank's," he says.

"I am."

"He is a great Canadian."

I stand there not knowing what to say. Agree with him or ask about the ambassadorship. Decide the diplomatic question is more interesting.

"You're the ambassador of Rock Lake?"

"Yes I am, sir. Drago Dumancic. At your service." He is in his late 60s I would think, speaks in a thick east-European accent; proceeds to tell me how he became an ambassador.

He immigrated to Canada from Yugoslavia in 1965, came with his wife, Nada. They were both in their early 20s; one of the lucky thousand or so that managed to emigrate from communist Yugoslavia each year.

He came to Canada after doing a blitz of embassies in Vienna (where he was working at the time as a bricklayer) and the Canadian embassy was the first to say he could come, so long as he paid his way.

When he arrived in Toronto, Drago was asked where he wanted to live. He and Nada had spent months reading up on Canada and Drago told the immigration official he wanted to see nature. All the rugged beautiful nature they had seen in photos, in the brochures the embassy had given him. Where should they go?

The immigration official suggested Port Arthur-Port William (now Thunder Bay.) He showed the couple photos. Drago said "Perfect."

And he says it *was* perfect, everything he had dreamed of while waiting to leave Yugoslavia. He became a member of the bricklayers union in Thunder Bay and moved around the country, "building Canada strong with masonry," he says.

Thirty years after arriving in Canada his knees gave out and Drago retired to Collingwood. During his first year of retirement he came to Algonquin Park for the first time. He arrived at Rock Lake in July and didn't leave until Thanksgiving.

There it was. The land he and Nada had gazed upon when they were a young couple, living in an apartment in Zagreb, looking at photos from Canadian travel brochures. Right here at Rock Lake.

The next year he was waiting at the gates when the campground opened in May.

After a few years Drago was made the ambassador of Rock Lake, an official, if unpaid, position granted by the Park to a veteran camper at each of the larger campgrounds.

Drago told those who visited the ambassador's residence where they could walk in the morning to see the best sunrises. Where to go fishing. Where to find the best fall foliage.

"I tell them it is a beautiful country," says Drago. "A beautiful country, yes."

———◆———

It is like a Sunday afternoon church social when the children come back from fishing. There are games of tag and water pistol contests. Beanbags get tossed into holes drilled into a large log. There are face painters and a clown who juggles fishing bobbers. An Ontario Parks bush-plane lands on the lake and starts to ferry children around for aerial tours of Algonquin Park.

Frank with the ambassador of Rock Lake, Drago Dumancic

Within minutes of the first plates of fried fish appearing, there is a line-up in front of Heinz and Frank that stretches almost to the shore. They work in front of cast-iron skillets, twenty fillets in a pan, moving from skillet to skillet down a line of barbecues, but they still can't keep up.

Someone shouts the children should go first. A man at the front of the line shouts: "Children will be OK. I'm freakin' starving." The line moves slowly.

After lunch there is a raffle. Each child had been given a roll of 50-50 tickets when they registered to go fishing. Numbers are called out until each child is a winner.

While it took two months to catch the rock bass, it took six to assemble the prizes. Heinz and Frank contacted every hardware store, sporting goods store, tee-shirt and dollar store in the Highlands. You probably didn't need any words modifying the word "store." If someone sold a thing, why, that thing would be perfect for the Family Fishing Week derby.

William won a canvas tackle box with spinners, leaders, hooks and weights already inside. He looked at a small Williams Wabler and I told him he would probably have a chance to use that one tomorrow.

We would be returning to Whitefish Lake in the morning. This time to go fishing for lake trout with Frank.

———◆———

Frank stared at the bus ticket in his hand and wondered again what to do with it.

Her name had been Marie and he followed her off the bus in Cobalt, asking if he could buy her supper. That was five days ago.

He had been sleeping on her couch, pretending each morning to sleep in and then feigning panic when he realized he had missed the bus to Timmins. He couldn't keep doing that.

He had married a woman in Timmins; met here there and they had two small boys. Two months ago she left, taking the boys with her. Frank came home from his shift one night and found the apartment cleared out. She hadn't left a note.

He was drinking pretty heavy so he didn't blame her that much for leaving. Wished she'd left a note.

He stared again at the bus ticket. The word Timmins in big block letters at the top.

He had gone fishing with one of Marie's boys the day before and they had done well. Michael. A good boy. Marie was lucky to have a family that lived with her.

When he had stared at the ticket long enough he walked to the Greyhound ticket booth and cashed it in. Used the money to buy groceries and fishing lures. Headed back to Marie's.

———◆———

The next morning my alarm goes off at five a.m. and I lie in my sleeping bag for a minute before it comes back to me. Where I am.

I un-zip the flap over the window of the tent and look out on Rock Lake, where the sun is just starting to climb over the tree-line. Not there yet. A thin red line that shimmers and undulates above the trees.

I poke William in the chest and he opens his eyes, rolls onto his stomach and looks out the window with me. We watch as the red line grows and grows, then disappears when the crown of the sun appears above the spruce.

For a few minutes the trees are awash in a golden light. Not a bright light. Not a white light. A light you can stare right into.

"Time to get up," I say. "Frank's going to meet us at the boat launch at six."

———◆———

Arriving at Whitefish Lake that morning is like arriving at a festival the day after it ends. The crowds are gone. The food and vendor booths are gone. The parking lot is empty, except for Frank's minivan.

The mayhem of the day before had been replaced by a calm and stillness all the more noticeable because of what had preceded. There was no convoy of boats by the shore this morning. No bush-planes landing and taking off.

Just Frank. Smoking a cigarette and sitting in the back seat of the Mirro Seaquest.

———◆———

William has never trolled before. He holds the trolling rod Frank gives him, with a good Penn reel attached, and you can tell he is uncertain about the weight. Fishing rods aren't supposed to be this heavy.

He watches as Frank puts a Williams Wabler on his line. Listens as Frank explains how you troll, how William can determine how much line he is letting out by counting the rotations of the line-guide, two rotations being a foot of line. Then he has to judge the angle of the line going into the water to figure out the depth.

"I'd say that were 'bout three to one," says Frank. "Every three feet you let out, it go down a foot. Look that way to you?"

William looks at the line. Rubs his chin. Says it looks that way to him as well.

"So I want you to have the lure at twenty-five feet. How much line ya gotta let out?"

William rubs his chin again: "Seventy-five feet."

"That's right. We'll make a fisherman outta you yet."

When Frank has the lure running at twenty-five feet he passes the rod to William. Starts to explain action. An almost identical speech to what I heard the first time I went trolling with him.

"You need to jerk your rod when you're trollin'," he says. "'At's called action."

Why is it called that?"

"Because . ... .it acts on the lure."

"That make sense."

"'Course it does. Don't matter what its called t'ough. You gotta jerk the rod when you troll. Otherwise you're goin' to set there all day catchin' nothin'."

Frank has started fishing and gives William a demonstration of various jerks.

"You don't want to pull the rod. You got to snap it. You can snap it quick like this," and Frank flicks his hands as though making a hockey wrist shot. "Sometimes you want to do a bunch of those jerks and wait. Sometimes you wanna do it a bit slower" — Frank flips his hands as though tossing a Frisbee — "you can do a bunch of those as well. Or just a few. T's all about the action."

William has been following along with Frank. Quick jerk of his rod. Slower jerk. Quick-slow. Slow-quick.

"How do I know what action to use?" he asks.

Frank stares at my son as though a promising student has just revealed himself to be the class dullard. A sad and wistful sort of look comes over his face before he says.

"Use t'one that's catchin' fish."

Sometimes I think God is a fisherman. Or likes pulling pranks on fishermen.

A prankster God like the prankster fishermen you run across from time to time; the ones who hide the fly of your tent with a rain storm coming; put Tobasco in the breakfast eggs; collapse a tarp full of water on your head.

Lots of prankster fishermen in this world, including Frank, who once left a lazy fishing guide behind on an island while fishing a large lake in the interior of Algonquin

Park. Frank took off with the alcohol as well, which probably had more to do with the screaming you heard across the lake that night.

There are too many odd, inexplicable, absurd, never-to-be-seen-again-things that happen during a fishing trip not to believe in some sort of intervention. In some prankster God. If the natural world had been left to spin and march on its own we would not be here.

All of which is to say — William is the only one to catch fish.

He catches two lakers. Neither is big, a little more than two pounds, but both are larger than any fish he has caught before. He hoots and hollers when the first fish is netted, about an hour after we have started trolling.

Frank shows him the deep-fork in the tail, the green-grey hues on the flanks, tells him that's how you know it's a lake trout.

"That's a nice fish," William says.

"That's a beautiful fish," Frank corrects.

Thirty minutes later, with both Frank and I furiously jerking our rods, William catches another laker. Frank puts the fish on the stringer and jokes about my son catching our shore lunch and now it's a good thing he's here otherwise we'd go hungry.

William laughs and says he'll catch a splake for us now. Wants to see what that fish looks like. Trout are beautiful fish. Almost as beautiful are Pumpkinseeds he says.

Pumpkinseeds are colorful pan-fish he catches regularly on the Rideau River back in Ottawa. The fish has orange and blue colouring, can look like a burning Jack-O-Lantern if the sun hits it properly. It's about the size of rock bass. The children in our neighbourhood clap and cheer whenever someone catches a Pumpkinseed from the dock down the street.

Twenty minutes later — and again, how does this happen

unless someone, somewhere has a sense of humour? — William turns to Frank and says the lakers seem to have gone.

"Can we fish for Pumpkinseeds now?"

"Why would you wanna do that?"

"I like looking at them."

Frank doesn't answer right away. My son may be the first person to sit in his boat and ask to go Pumpkinseed fishing.

"Sure," he says. "There's a spot near the dock we can try on the way back."

———◆———

Although we catch no more fish it turns into a beautiful day on Whitefish Lake. The sun refracts off high cliffs, lighting the red granite so it looks like ingots of gold. No wonder the Algonquin thought this lake was magical. The Algonquin of Pikwakanagan still hold their annual pow-wow on the shores of Whitefish Lake.

We go for our shore lunch, on an island not far from the cliffs and watch a tern diving for fish. The bird circles and dips, making elaborate patterns in the sky, an aerial show that seems put on for our entertainment; sitting as we are only thirty feet away.

The show always ends with a sudden dive, no clue it is coming, an elevator-cable-snapping dive that ends with a splash of water and the bird re-emerging a few seconds later with a fish. William yells "boom" each time it happens.

Once, the tern surfaced with a fish larger than it and we watched it fly unsteadily to the shore, like a crippled plane, just managing to touch down before the trout slipped out its beak.

We troll for another hour after lunch, but we are already happy with the day and pack it in after that. On the way back to the boat launch we stop and fish for Pumpkinseeds.

———◆———

LESSON SIX
How to Raise Good Kids and Spot Bad Ones

"I can't take credit for any of my kids. I was drinking when they were growing up and you can't take a drunk seriously. 'Specially if he's talking about how to raise kids.

"But I've been a sober a long time. Had a lot of years to think about what I did wrong. So maybe I know what you shouldn't do.

"Shouldn't ride kids all the time. I'll tell you that. Riding a kid, tellin' 'em what to do all the time, that's normally done by people who'd like to ride adults but they can't. So they ride kids.

"I don't think you should run around telling 'em how special they are, though, 'cuz you'd be lyin' to 'em. Most kids are pretty much the same. And kids know that. They spend most of their time with other kids, right? They know they ain't no different.

"Besides, kids don't need to be buttered up. They ain't adults. A kid that's been told his whole life how special he is, that's going to be a bad kid."

"The best thing ya can do for a kid is not be in in a hurry. If a kid is with someone that don't want to leave, he knows that. And if that's how a kid thinks 'bout ya, you'll probably be all right."

THE
LAST GUIDE'S
GUIDE

We spend one last night at our campsite, a picture-perfect Algonquin Park night. One with a crescent moon suspended over spruce hills. The sky a splash of stars you could look at for hours.

As we crawl into our sleeping bags a loon starts calling out for its mate. William says the sound reminds him of train whistles but he isn't sure why. He doesn't think they sound alike at all. Why would that be?

When I think of a good way of answering the question, I look over, but he is already asleep.

———◆———

The next day we break camp early and drive to Whitney. Frank is guiding this day and we said our goodbyes yesterday. We have a late breakfast at the Algonquin Lunch Bar. Go to the Madawaska Bait and Tackle Shop to buy ice for the cooler.

Matt Fitzpatrick had moved his store to Whitney earlier in the year, when a storefront became available on Highway 60, not far from the Twin E. Things had gone well enough for Fitzpatrick's father to even move to the Highlands, to help out his son.

His father not only worked in the store from time to time, but had started selling fiberglass canoes in the back of the bait store. His father had been making canoes for many years, but now that he had beaten cancer he was turning it into full-time work.

"He loves it up here. He's like a kid again," said Fitzpatrick. "We go fishing a couple times a week."

"Things have worked out well for you."

"Yep. I should have run away years ago."

I buy some ice for the cooler. Some water and cans of pop. A woman rang through the purchase and I thought the bait-and-tackle shop must be doing quite well if Fitzpatrick now had employees, but before we left he brought the woman a coffee and hugged her and I knew that wasn't what had happened.

William took him to the Jeep to show him the lake trout he caught. Fitzpatrick looked suitably impressed.

"And Frank didn't catch anything?"

"Nothing," yelled William.

"I am so glad you dropped by."

————◆————

On the drive to Ottawa William peers out his window and asks questions — "How many logs do you think are in that lumber yard?" "How can they be so sure it's the first Polish settlement?" "We've seen the Bonnechere Caves, right?"

Then the land starts to drop off, become level, the forests became plowed fields, the trees tall stalks of corn. We drive through Renfrew and then onto the Trans-Canada Highway. By the time we reach Arnprior, he is reading a book.

He only looks out his window one more time, to ask when we will be home.

————◆————

As we make the drive I think of Matt Fitzpatrick. He is not the first person to run away to the Algonquin Highlands. Tom Thomson was a runaway. Lillian Kates was a runaway.

E.B. White, author of *Charlotte's Web,* couldn't stop running away. Twice in his literary career White sold everything he owned and fled New York City for a life in the Algonquin Highlands. The second time, he bought a boys' summer camp, not far from the West Gate of the Park.

The most successful runaway was probably Archie Belaney, better known by his alias of Grey Owl. Belaney was an English schoolboy from Sussex, England who came to Northern Ontario as a teenager, telling everyone he was an Apache from the Dakotas. He trapped regularly in the Highlands and later became a famous writer and conservationist.

Everyone fell for the sham, which is astonishing to this day. From Algonquin chiefs to Oxford dons, no one thought to ask Grey Owl any hard questions. Like where he learned to read and write. Whether there was another Apache on the planet with a nose like that.

The *North Bay Nugget* exposed the sham the day Belaney died in 1938, a story the newspaper had been sitting on for three years. Today, his reputation is mixed.

Although it was one breath-taking run.

———◆———

Frank doesn't spend much time wondering why an English schoolboy would run away, move to the Highlands and pretend to be an Apache from the Dakotas.

There is a lake Frank used to fish from time to time, Dickson Lake. It took three portages to get into it from the far eastern arm of Opeongo Lake, so he didn't bother with it all that often. Although it was part of a good, week-long loop from Opeongo up to White Partridge Lake and back, so occasionally he did.

For years there was an abandoned log cabin on the lake. A couple of additions had been added to the cabin so it was more like a farmhouse. And in the middle of that cabin sat a piano.

The piano was there a long time, as no one knew how to pillage it the way everything else in the farmhouse had been pillaged when the homesteaders left. Not a small piano either, like you might see in the corner of a tavern, which would be remarkable enough.

This was one large piano. Shaped like a kidney. With a top that popped. A concert grand, someone had called it one time.

One night, when he was camping on the lake, Frank

Archie Belaney, early conservationist and
fake Apache, feeding a baby beaver

examined the piano in detail, to see where it had been disassembled before being portaged in. He looked for nearly an hour but never found any signs.

That piano had come in whole.

What people took with them when they ran away; how they expected it to work for them; why they ran in the first place; Frank had stopped asking questions like that a long time ago.

———◆———

We get home shortly before six. William helps me take out the bags and fishing rods, the pop-up tent and cooler.

I walk down the driveway carrying the cooler, feeling the way I have always felt when coming back from Algonquin Park.

We've just driven the wrong way.

Year Three

Late last night I had me a dream,
I was out fishin' in a whiskey stream,
Baited my hook with apple-jack,
Threw out a drink, drug a gallon back.
(Done pretty good till the creek run dry.
I give the fish back to the finance guy.)

— Woody Guthrie, "Talking Fishing Blues"

Strap yourself
To the tree with roots
You ain't goin' nowhere

— Bob Dylan, "You Ain't Goin' Nowhere"

◆ 6 ◆

A bad winter — The Opeongo Colony Road — Stone fences — What you need — A heat-wave in Whitney

The winter of 2013-14 was a long one for most of Canada. The January thaw lasted only days this time, only hours in some places. It was the winter when most Canadians heard the term "polar vortex" for the first time.

By February 26th, Hamilton had been under a cold alert for 46 days. Toronto had been under a similar alert for 36 days. There was snow on the ground in both cities for nearly one-hundred-and-twenty days.

That winter snowfall records were set in Kenora, Calgary, Windsor and Red Deer. In early March, Environment Canada reported the three-month period from December-February had been the coldest since national weather statistics started being compiled in 1948.

On New Year's Day in Ottawa, the temperature dropped more than 24 degrees in 24 hours, setting up a cold-spell that ran until late March. The average temperature in the nation's capital for the month of February was minus-twenty-one Celsius.

In the Algonquin Highlands, so much snow fell people stopped using back doors and side-entrances and kept only one path cleared to their homes. The cold was so bitter even new model cars had to have their batteries plugged in

What You Need to Make It Through a Bad Winter

When I saw Frank after the never-ending winter of 2013-14, I asked him what you needed to get through a bad winter. Here is his answer, the twelve items listed in the order in which he gave them.

1. Woolen toque
2. Snow tires
3. Chaga tea
4. Two pair of long underwear
5. Good-size freezer
6. Music
7. Snowshoes (wooden, gut-strung, check garage sales)
8. Rubberized boots (you can save a lot of money by buying boots that will keep your feet dry, one size larger than normal, and doubling up on woolen socks)
9. Road salt
10. Good winter jacket (again, you can save a lot of money by buying a water-repellant coat and doubling up on sweaters. You don't need a parka as you already have the toque.)
11. Word-puzzle books
12. Decent snow shovel (buy a good one. good chance winter is coming next year.)

THE
LAST GUIDE'S
GUIDE

overnight, to have any chance of starting in the morning.

It was worse in the prairies, which suffered through its third consecutive cold winter. In Winnipeg the temperature was minus-30 Celsius or lower for thirty days. In Saskatoon there was snow on the ground for six months, again a national record.

As for Regina, it is a wonder anyone emerged alive from the winter of 2013-14. According to Environment Canada, on a few days that winter, the city was colder than the surface of Mars.

——◆——

Frank didn't go fishing come Opening Day. Most of the lakes in Algonquin Park were still frozen and any that weren't had ice hugging the shore, so you would have had to push your canoe out with one leg on the ice, the other in the boat, so you wouldn't go completely in when the ice gave.

While Frank did that a few times when he was a young man, he wasn't doing it this year. He had already phoned Jack Mihell and told him not to come.

The disappearance of spring caused a certain languor to take hold that year. People in Ottawa walked around looking exhausted and jittery; in their eyes was a far-away stare that was part ennui, or part despair, it was difficult to tell. It seemed to depend on the light.

It was hard that spring to get motivated to do much of anything, to stay on any task. All sense of urgency evaporated, because if one immoveable reference point could disappear, then maybe they all could. We were suddenly living in a world without boundaries or reasonable expectations.

Frank's unfinished guidebook sat at the edge of my desk, in about the same place (comparatively speaking, although the space was different) as the stack of maps and magazines he kept on his kitchen table. If Frank was not reaching over to grab *The Canoe Routes of Algonquin Park*, I was not reaching over to grab *The Last Guide's Guide*.

Not worried about it that much. Not in any particular hurry. We would pick it up later.

Maybe what happened in the spring of 2014 was an example of how messed up people would become if a real season ever did disappear. Before long it would seem like we were living in one big opium den.

————◆————

While I waited to return to Whitney I worked on the guide-book as best I could. Now that there were no deadlines. No sense of urgency. No fishing trip planned.

So not much at all. Sunday mornings were normal. For a couple hours and then onto something else.

It was on one of those Sunday mornings, though, that I came across the story of Thomas French. And learned, finally, why Wilno is Canada's first Polish settlement (something I had always wondered about and that had never been explained to me in any way that made sense.)

Why the Opeongo Line never got past Bark Lake. And why there are so many sad-looking stone fences, abandoned and overgrown, in the Algonquin Highlands.

————◆————

Five years into his job as road agent for the Opeongo Colony Road, Thomas French was beginning to feel like the front man for a crooked card game. A shill for some bottles-tilted-backwards, ring-toss game.

Worst part about that feeling was knowing he'd brought every sucker into the carnival tent.

In his defence, French didn't realize how crooked the game would be. How do you know about anything, really,

Frank in his ice-fishing hut

until you have lived through it, until you have experienced it? It's a bit of faith on everyone's part until that happens, right?

Particularly if you're talking about land, which you have no sense of whatsoever until you've put down roots. Or tried to put down roots. Which was rather the problem.

French had written a pamphlet. One of the first things he did after being hired as road agent. *Information for Intending Settlers on the Ottawa and Opeongo Road* it was called and he had been proud of it at the time. A good piece of writing, he thought.

Much of the information for the pamphlet had been supplied by the government of Upper Canada, as French lived in Mount Shannon, at the base of the Highlands. He had taken trips through the Highlands, but again, what do you know about land until you put down roots?

Only now, five years later, did phrases like "fertile agricultural land," and "wealth of opportunities," come back to haunt him.

The land here was so poor it was all French could do most days to maintain the mien of a knowledgeable, unflappable, road agent — what he was sure both settlers and employer expected of him — instead of breaking down and crying.

Every day French would watch settler families clearing their land, sometimes as many as five or six men trying to roll a granite boulder from a field, their backs tight against the rock, pushing with their feet, taking short, gaunt steps backwards, looking for all the world like plow-horses in steer.

Most of them were Polish. His pamphlet had been translated into their language. By whom, he had no idea.

But every single settler out there breaking his back in a field had two things in common. They spoke a language French didn't understand. And they were here because of his pamphlet.

———◆———

The settlers were resourceful and hard working and quickly found a use for the rocks they moved. They started building stone fences.

The fences marked the boundaries of the one hundred acres that would be theirs one day and the fences became ever more elaborate and ornate, as more rocks were moved. In time the fences became a source of pride for the settlers, who had little else to show for their time along the Opeongo Colony Road.

The settlers had conditions to meet before they were given clear title and deed to their land. Legend has it French saw those stone fences and one day thought of a way he could make amends for what he had done.

He wrote a letter to the government, explaining his idea. Why he felt it was the right thing to do. Not only for the settlers, but for the government of Upper Canada as well, as the Opeongo Line stood a good chance of failing, being abandoned, if something was not done soon to reward the settlers for their hard work.

As he wrote, his old gift for rhetoric came back. He asked the government what the difference might be, the substantive difference, between un-deeded land grants and indentured servitude.

He later took that part out. He still needed a job.

———◆———

French waited nearly two years for a reply. In that time he gave up answering questions from the settlers, who all wanted to know when they might be given clear title to their land.

French explained that the necessary forms had been completed. The acreage of cleared land listed, along with any other land improvements.

It was now in the hands of the government. All they could do was wait.

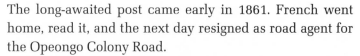

The long-awaited post came early in 1861. French went home, read it, and the next day resigned as road agent for the Opeongo Colony Road.

It would be many months before the position could be filled and in that time the road was more or less abandoned. A corduroy road had reached Bark Lake and that would be the end of it.

The post that arrived the day before French resigned was waiting for the new lands agent when he arrived later that year, sitting on a desk with no other papers or official documents.

The land agent unfolded the letter. The short note said stone fences would not be considered as land improvements by the government of Upper Canada.

By mid-July I had still not made it to Whitney. The disappearance of spring — and the disappearance of our spring fishing trip — had badly delayed the guidebook. Some days I looked at it, sitting there on my desk, and didn't see paper anymore. I saw stone fences.

I got busy at the same time. A summer series I was doing for the *Ottawa Sun* had last-minute problems with copyright on some archival photos, and I suddenly found myself chasing down archivists at the National Library Canada, all of whom seemed to be on holidays.

My children were busy with soccer and summer camps, my wife had a project of her own on the go, an *Ottawa Citizen* feature about Jonathan Pitre, a young boy suffering from a rare and life-limiting skin disease (her photos for the story would win a National Newspaper Award the following spring.)

It occurred to me that summer that nature is not the only thing that abhors a vacuum. Work feels pretty much the same way.

My days got busier and busier. The guidebook kept dropping down on my list of things to do.

————◆————

Frank phoned a few times to ask when I was coming up and I never had an answer for him any better than "soon as I clear a few things off my desk, Frank." Whenever I said it I looked at my desk and was grateful he never asked how many things might be sitting there.

I bought a boat that spring as well, a small cuddy, and had planned on spending time on the Rideau River. By mid-July I had taken the boat out once.

Most days I sat at my desk and couldn't decide what made me feel guiltier: the boat or the book.

————◆————

Not being able to find the time to do what you want to do is not a new problem for me. It was a modern dilemma I had been trying to find the answer to for years.

How exactly do you carve out time for the things you like doing, when you're so busy doing the things that need to be done? Or what others have decided needs to be done. Or you better do right now, before things get complicated and ugly.

Again, it was mid-July when I started asking those questions. And maybe it was the way I phrased it this time that made something click.

What you want to do. What you need to do.

A conversation I had with Frank. I reached across my desk and started flipping through my notes for the guidebook. Found it near the bottom. A transcript from an interview on Head Lake more than two years ago. One of our first interviews.

We had been talking about his tackle box, Frank telling me what you needed to have in a tackle box. The "five lures you'd be an idiot not to own" and I had asked what else you need, in general, to have a good life.

I sat back and read what he had said.

———◆———

"I think what you need depends 'n how old you are. What an old man needs and a young man needs, that's always going to be two different things.

"When I was young I drank a lot. I go to the meetings now and everyone has a story of how they stopped drinkin'. People remember the date and everythin. I do too.

"People 'member when they started, too. Sneakin' their daddy's homemade wine, drinkin' a mickey behind some hockey arena. Me, I have no idea. I can't 'member not drinkin'.

"(So I) used to think I needed alcohol. But I didn't. It was just something I made up in my head. A lot of the stuff you think you need is like that. Made-up stuff.

"There's some real stuff you need, but not much. Depends how old you are. What you're doing. It's always a moving target.

"The stuff you like is different. Ever notice that? If you like fishin' you're probably always going to like fishin'. Always going to like readin'. Always goin' to like music. Stuff you like stays with you."

———◆———

Stuff you like stays with you. Stuff you need is a moving target.

I sat in my study and tried to figure out where that fell apart. Where the mistake was. It seemed too simple.

And yet most of us *do* spend much of our adult lives pursuing the things we have convinced ourselves we need. Unaware, until it happens, that what we need doesn't stand

still. It will change tomorrow. After the doctor's appointment. After the passing on the street of your future spouse.
After the next e-mail.

The stuff you like is different. It's a part of you that
doesn't go away.

I looked and looked but couldn't see the mistake.

———◆———

Frank answered on the second ring.

"There you are."

"What are you doing this weekend?"

"Fishin'."

"Mind if I come up?"

"You should. You wuz the one I was thinkin' of goin'
with."

———◆———

There was a drought in Whitney when I arrived. It hadn't
rained in the Highlands for thiry-six days, going back to
June 19, when a light drizzle had skiffed through town late
in the afternoon.

It had been thirty degrees Celsius or higher for twenty-
six of those days. Some in the village claimed there hadn't
been a cloud in the sky since the drought started, but no
one thought to start cloud searching back in June so no one
could say with certainty if that were true. Seemed true.

Certainly it was an unbearable heat that went on day
after day and after more than a month of of it people in the
Highlands were starting to act listless and slightly crazy.

Heat waves can have that affect on people wherever they
occur, but it was worse in the Highlands, where historical
weather records have it snowing every month of the year
and some men only own work shirts.

The Freshmart grocery took to keeping a clerk near the
frozen food coolers in back of the store, not guarding them
exactly, just having someone nearby to remind people that

if they keep their head in the coolers for longer than a minute they really should be pulling something out with them when they re-emerge.

Most gift shops decided to shut right down in the afternoon, not wanting to spend air-conditioning money for sales that didn't justify the expense, a decision that surprised a lot of people as the gift shops had seemed quite popular that August, with many locals coming back day after day to consider purchases.

The ice cream store at Lake of Two Rivers Campground ran out of ice cream four times. The bears stopped coming to the dump. It was a heat wave of historic proportions.

———◆———

The night before I drove to Whitney I talked to Frank on the phone and asked how he was coping in the heat. I got a strange answer.

"No problems here. I know how to beat a heat wave."

"You know how to beat a heat wave?" I said.

"Right on."

"How have you done that?"

"I'll show you when you get here."

———◆———

The drive to Whitney was about as bad as any I've made to the Algonquin Highlands. Made winter driving seem easy and I don't think any of my father's cars would have made it.

With the air conditioning on full, I sweated the entire way. I genuinely wondered if I would make it up some hills, looking at my heat gauge not with concern but fear. I burnt my hand on the rear panel of the Jeep while getting gas in Barry's Bay.

Yet when I passed Barry's Bay and phoned Frank, to tell him I was half an hour away, he answered sounding as refreshed as though the sun was hidden behind thick clouds and he was on his first cup of coffee of the day.

"I'll see you in a bit then," he said. "I'm out in the driveway."

"You're working outside on a day like this?"

"Nah, I'm just in the driveway. Been here most of the day."

"Why in the world would you be outside today if you don't need to be?"

"I'll see you when you get here."

———◆———

The heat rays shimmering on the highway as I drove were so close and so plentiful I kept thinking dust was blowing across the road. I'm not sure of the adjective or phrase that would best describe the day: sweltering, blistering, steaming, volcanic, time-to-move-to-Iqaluit.

Yet sure enough, when I pulled into Frank's driveway he was outside waiting for me. I walked to where he was and stared down.

"Where'd you get the water?"

"Galeairy Lake. I take the fishing boat to the launch and back 'er right in."

"Why don't you leave the water in the fishing boat?"

"I prefer a canoe."

I laughed at what I was seeing – frank lying in a canoe filled with water. His common-sense solution to beating a heat wave. Plenty of boats in the Algonquin Highlands. Plenty of cold water. Just combine them.

Frank had been the only one to think of it.

"What do you do when the water warms up?"

"Go back to the boat launch."

Of course.

Frank demonstrating how to beat a heat wave
in the Algonquin Highlands

· 7 ·

The Great Bass Dump of 1910 — Talking about money — Useful skills — Catching a big fish — Looking at maps — The short and happy political life of Frank Kuiack

Because of the heat wave we aren't going to fish for trout this trip. Trout is a cold-water fish that might have been jumping dams right then trying to get a little further north. Bass, on the other hand, if we fished them right, might be an easy catch.

Even with that being said, when Frank suggested we go bass fishing I was surprised. There was a time he never would have considered it.

Bass are not native to Algonquin Park. They are a warm-water fish that were introduced only a few years after the Park was created. It was an interventionist act for which some of the old guides never forgave either the provincial or federal governments.

Both were guilty of bass propagation: the federal Ministry of Fisheries, and the Ontario Department of Crown Lands. Bass lovers the pair of them.

Not to mention the hatchery in Newcastle, Ontario, a private business that raised bass by the hundreds of thousands — fry right up to catchable fish — and sent them by train to lakes across Ontario.

That's how bass were "introduced" in the Highlands. A train would stop by the side of a lake, metal cans from the Newcastle hatchery or the Bay of Quinte hatchery would be taken off, the cans opened, the fish dumped, the cans re-loaded and the train would continue on its way.

That was bass stocking in the early days, a slap-dash game that not only the government played, but any rich Sport who wanted to place an order with a hatchery.

The lakes along the Grand Trunk rail-line in Algonquin Park were the first lakes to be stocked with bass — Cache Lake, Rock Lake, Smoke Lake — and Sports had as much to do with that as any government.

American sports loved black bass. So they would have the hatchery cans loaded on the train, pay the conductor to stop on his way to the Highland Inn, and then introduce the bass to whatever lake they had stopped at.

Most of the guides didn't care for the fish. They would fish for bass when the Sports paid them, but couldn't understand why anyone would prefer bass to trout, the fish they had been catching all their lives.

In comparison to trout, bass were ugly and poor tasting and if you let in bass, where would it all stop? Would we be introducing pike next?

It almost worked out for the guides. For more than a decade every attempt at bass stocking in the Park failed, or was such a meager success it didn't seem like a serious problem that would last.

But then in 1910 a train stopped beside Cache Lake, metal barrels from the Bay of Quinte hatchery were taken off, and 10,000 bass were "introduced" to the lake.

People have been catching bass in Algonquin Park ever since.

———◆———

But Frank had suggested bass fishing and I sat at his kitchen table wondering if I had just heard that right.

"Bass fishing? Is that what you just said?"

"I did," says Frank. "I know a good lake we can go to."

"When did you start bass fishing?"

"I've always fished bass. Jeepers, you know that. My very first clients were bass fishermen."

"They were paying you. When did you start doing it for free?"

"Bass ain't a bad fish," he says, almost sheepishly. "You just got to know how to fish 'em."

——◆——

The next morning we don't drive to Algonquin Park but to a boat launch on Galeairy Lake, where Frank puts the Mirro Seaquest into the water and we head down the north shore.

We have not left as early as usual, a concession to the short drive to the boat launch and the motor-boat that will take us to the first portage. The sky is an early-dawn grey as we travel down the lake. The mist is already starting to burn off and there is a tern in the sky, already fishing. Half way down the north shore we pass a sign saying we have just entered Algonquin Park.

Although everyone called the fish "black bass" when it was stocked more than a hundred years ago, there were two kinds of bass introduced (or dumped off the train) to the Highlands: smallmouth and largemouth. We will be going for largemouth bass today.

Galeairy Lake is a large lake with two arms (it was called Long Lake for decades, until the Ontario government decided there were too many Long Lakes in the province and changed the name.) We travel down the western arm, past Farm Bay, where Frank and I have fished for speckles before.

The Ottawa-Arnprior-and-Parry-Sound Railway used to follow the shoreline here, and you can see what looks like a line through the forest, of smaller trees and cedar, where the rail-line must have been.

When we reach the end of the western arm we beach the boat and head down a short portage. A few minutes later we are standing by the shoreline of Aubrey Lake. Frank goes to get the canoe.

———◆———

A few minutes after that we are bass fishing, casting surface lures toward little channels of water cutting through bull-rushes along the shore. These channels are where largemouth like to hide, their tails twitching back and forth, keeping their bodies stationed between the rushes and the open water.

Most times a largemouth will hit within seconds of a lure landing in the water. Bass lures are sold and marketed these days with all sorts of retrieve — surface, deep, middle, suspending — but the truth is, if a largemouth doesn't hit shortly after you cast, it probably won't.

So landing the lure in the right spot is crucial. Frank flips his into the channels as easily and precisely as an NBA all-star making a thee-point shot.

That nothing-but-net swooshing sound of a good three-point basket is also close to what you hear when a largemouth takes a lure. The fish doesn't bite the lure so much as suck it into its mouth. The sound you hear is nothing but lure.

Which means you can hear the bass attack before you feel the strike in the rod. A form of anticipation you don't get with trout. You wait to hear the fish.

———◆———

As we cast our lures Frank tells me he has been thinking about the guidebook and thinks we may have a problem. All the stuff we've talked about the past three years: fishing, shore lunches, plants you should know, good things

Frank and Matt Fitzpatrick

and bad things and how to spot the difference between them, what was the sense of recording any of that stuff if you didn't spend some time talking about money?

How to make it. How to keep it in your pockets. Why, you'd be almost foolish if you started yammering on about other stuff before you talked about money. People either want more of it, or they don't have enough of it, and if you don't have enough of it, well, that was your whole life right there. Money. It takes over everything.

"It's 'cuz most people don't look at money the right way," he says, the canoe drifting a little as he rolls a cigarette.

"What do you mean?"

"Well, a hundred dollars is a hundred dollars, right? You agree with me on that?"

"Sure."

"Well, most people don't. Most people care how they make that hundred dollars. Care an awful lot. Shouldn't be that way. You can make a hundred dollars working in an office or you can make a hundred dollars cleaning up road-kill for the MNR (Ministry of Natural Resources.) It's the same hundred dollars, right?"

"It *is* the same hundred dollars."

"Well then, why am I the only one cleaning up road kill?"

———◆———

As Frank talks about money we continue casting plugs toward the bull-rushes, let them sit a few seconds, give a few small jerks of the rod, then bring the plug back and cast again.

I still have trouble believing we are bass fishing. How exactly do you change a life-long bias? Biases tend to get more entrenched the older you get, but here was Frank, casting plugs toward a weedy shoreline, hoping to catch a fish he once wouldn't go after unless, literally, you paid him.

It is not quite the historic concession of the Northern Ireland Peace Accords, but for a Polish fisherman from the Algonquin Highlands, a man who used to consider the "bass dump of 1910" a dark day in Canadian history, it is pretty close.

There had been some other changes recently. Just as surprising.

After using steel line on his trolling rods for seventy years, late last year Frank switched to Fireline, a special monofilament line from Berkeley, telling me – and I needed him to repeat it – that it worked better.

Jumping into a mini-van still felt strange, after a decade spent jumping into Frank's Dodge Dakota truck. His radio was turned to a country station yesterday that played songs released after *Achy Breaky Heart*. Now I was sitting in a canoe with him, bass fishing.

To each change, when asked about it, Frank had a pat answer: "It works better." Occasionally he would add: "And it's cheaper." Or: "And it's easier to carry."

It dawned on me that Frank doesn't have biases or prejudices in the traditional sense, as a learned emotion or an irrational conclusion. Like so much else in his life, Frank's actions are governed almost entirely by utility.

If something works it is good. If it doesn't, then it's bad.

And he never stops testing what is good and what is bad, the way most people do, who, once they have decided something is good don't think about it much after that (which explains Rolling Stones fans after 1978.)

Frank keeps testing what he believes. After seventy years, bass just passed.

————◆————

While we fish Frank keeps talking about money, saying people usually find a way to make money more complicated than it needs to be, when it's actually pretty simple.

Knowing how to fish, for example, is the same thing as having money in your pockets. Fish equals money. That's how it works.

The same way trees equal money. And minnows equal money. And backhoes and trap-lines and cottages built in the middle of nowhere on a stagnant lake can equal money, so long as the cottages are near Algonquin Park and can be billed as an eco-retreat.

There are all sorts of ways of making money in this world. You just need to look around for them.

Like Basil Sawyer, who gave up guiding when he discovered a company in Toronto was willing to pay good money for scrub pine. Or stunt pine as some people called it. Small trees that never grow above your kneecap, a useless little tree that turned out to be perfect for making Christmas wreaths.

The company in Toronto bought as much scrub pine as Sawyer could ship. There's no end apparently to the holiday spirit in Canada's largest city. After a few years Sawyer changed the name of the tree to Princess Pine and managed to charge even more.

Before long Sawyer gave up guiding and started driving around the Algonquin Highlands with a flat-bed truck that had a weigh-scale affixed to the bed, buying scrub pine in the autumn from anyone willing to pick it, after trout season had finished, the bush camps weren't open yet for the winter and there wasn't much else going on.

Sawyer became rich from princess pine. So rich he started to lose sleep over things like shipping rates and Japanese competition, Japan being a country that had lots of stunt pine for some reason, a fact of nature Sawyer couldn't quite fathom.

It was probably the worry that killed him. Sawyer died of a heart attack while driving back from North Bay, where he had gone to inspect a shipment of princess pine sitting at the rail-yard.

The Difference Between Money and Numbers

"The last vehicle I bought was a mini-van. I like mini-vans. They're good on gas. Can tow a boat easy enough. People who need a big honkin' pickup truck to go fishin', I don't bother with that stuff anymore.

"(I bought) the van at a dealer in Bancroft, told him I was looking for a new vehicle. I asked what his best price was for a van I was looking at. Sales guy said he might be able to take a thousand dollars off the sticker price.

"Then I asked him about my truck (for a trade) and he had a look at it. Guy turned all sad on me. Kept sayin' "high mileage" like it was some sort of disease. Tells me I won't get much on a trade-in.

"So I get his best price for the trade-in and for the van and then I leave and go to my bank. I withdraw two-thousand dollars less than that guy's best price. Put the money in a gym bag.

"I go to the dealership and find the sales guy sittin' at his desk.

"(I ask him) 'Twenty-one-five, that's your best deal?' The guy says, 'Rock-bottom Frank. And only because it's you.'

"I open the bag and dump the money on his desk. Nineteen-thousand — and -five-hundred dollars. In twenties. He was so startled he swore. I won't repeat what he said.

"I told him: 'You take the money, I take the van.

"That's what happened. I knew it would. In this world there's numbers and then there's money sitting on your desk. They ain't the same thing."

THE
LAST GUIDE'S
GUIDE

That would be another good thing for people to know. There are many ways in the world to make money. But if Toronto is involved in any sort of way, it probably isn't worth it.

———◆———

"I can't believe we're bass fishing."

"It ain't that strange."

"Not that strange? You used to say bass ruined all the good trout lakes in Algonquin."

"That's not true. There's lots of lakes they can't get into."

"That's what you used to say, though. Most people, the older they get, the harder it is to change."

"I don't know 'bout that. Being old don't mean you can't change. Being stupid means you can't change."

———◆———

Frank tosses his lure to within two feet of the bulrushes. As we watch the lure float on the water it disappears. Just vanishes. Nothing has broken the surface of the water but that lure is gone.

Frank pulls back on his rod and you can see the line going taut, start to quiver like a plucked guitar string. The tip of the rod starts to jerk at the same time, like the tine in his alarm clock when it's 4:30 in the morning.

A second later we see the bass. Or its mouth at least, brought to the surface after it has sucked in the lure and Frank has jerked his rod; the fish caught by surprise. Then it dives, so quickly and with such force we don't see its back fin, the way you normally would.

"My Lawd, did you see that?" says Frank.

"I did. You've got a good one there."

"I may have a great one there."

Frank starts to reel in line. Not smoothly the way he normally would but in jerky motions, fighting to get his hand to the top of the arc, then dropping on the downward stroke as though a great weight has fallen. I have pulled in my line and watch him work for a minute. I don't think he was able to make ten rotations of the reel in that minute.

Then the line suddenly goes slack and Frank's hands career out of control, the line spinning madly for a second because of the sudden loss of tension. It spools out of the cage and comes dangerously close to becoming a tangled mess.

Frank rarely swears. The next words out his mouth are: "Shit. Shit. Shit."

"It's coming for the boat?"

"Either that or she's about to jump. She can't jump. I'm not ready."

The fish jumps. And we see it for the first time. A bass so big it seems to float for a minute above the water, floating and spinning and flying through the air, gills and fins and water rolling in a lazy double-gainer. Then a splash and re-entry that throws up so much water I feel a few drops, sitting in a canoe thirty feet away.

Now it was my turn.

"My lord."

"That's right. My lawd. My lawd. That's a fish."

"Do you still have it?"

"I'll tell you in a second," and Frank keeps reeling in his line, showing no sign of tension yet. The bass may have already flipped the lure. Five seconds. Ten seconds. That fish is gone. Fifteen seconds. Long gone.

Then the line goes taut so quickly it pulls Frank forward in his seat.

"There she is. All right, let's start that again."

Frank works the fish for the next twenty minutes and never seems to have so much as one easy rotation of the reel. The fish fights every up-stroke. Twists and changes the angle on every down-stroke,

It makes one more run, not toward the canoe this time,

but to a patch of dead-heads and submerged trees near the southern shore. Frank needs to keep the fish in open water or his line will surely be cut on the deadheads.

He reels furiously to keep up with the fish, then pulls back on his rod when the tension has come back to his line. The fish jumps one last time. It had come to within two feet of the sunken trees.

Ten minutes later Frank has the bass swimming beside the canoe, twitching only slightly to keep its place in the water. Objects in the water are always hard to judge, as to exactly what size they might be, but that fish seemed to run from one seat in the canoe to the yoke, which would be close to four feet. When I read up on bass records later that summer I figure it had to be less than that. The water must have distorted it somehow.

But that is one monster fish beside the canoe. Fat the way a big bass would be this time of year, not lean and snake-like, the way a pike would have looked. Frank stares at the fish for a moment, then reaches down and picks it up by the gills, one smooth and continuous movement of his arm — in water, up with fish — takes pliers he is holding in his other hand, deftly removes the lure and slides the fish back into the water.

Let's go.

The bass stays beside the canoe for only a few seconds, so brief was the time Frank had it out of the water, so brief the time needed to re-orient itself. Then the tail of the big fish gives a flip large enough to churn the water around the canoe and it's gone.

"You didn't want to keep that one?"

"Nah," says Frank. "A fish that big won't taste any good. Might as well leave it here."

I sit there in disbelief until Frank says:

"Are you gonna fish or what?"

———◆———

Five minutes later I catch a bass coming out the same channel, a little more than a pound, then ten minutes later another one about the same size.

Frank catches two more as well, one a little larger than mine and one a little smaller. A third bass, that looks bigger than all of them, flips the lure just as Frank has it within five feet of the canoe.

A lot of activity in an hour, but then the fish must have moved on from that channel because it goes cold and after that we go for our shore lunch.

Frank fillets one of the small bass I have caught and when we are sitting on a rock with plates of food on our knees he asks if I can taste it, the difference between bass and trout.

"It ain't as strong tasting as trout," he says. "It's almost sweet."

He shakes his head. He didn't expect that either.

———◆———

As we eat our lunch Frank continues to talk about money, saying again that the trick is to not complicate things. A hundred dollars is a hundred dollars.

And diversify when you can. People with careers, those are people stuck knowing only one way to make money. Which is like being trapped. Except you were the one who put yourself there, so maybe "trapped" isn't the right word.

When Frank started guiding he could see right away that the Sports had other needs. Within a week he was bringing firewood to sell them. Frogs and minnows. When he was old enough he brought moonshine his father made on their stove back home, using maple syrup as the base so it had a fine, textured brown hue to it, a colour that reminded the Sports of bourbon whiskey and was hugely popular in the camp.

Even though the Sports acted like rabid dogs when they drank the moonshine, Frank still sold it to them. Because

A shore lunch in the 1940s

the money the Sports pressed into his hands for moonshine was the same as what was pressed for the fish. The wood. The frogs.

The more ways you have of making money, the more you're willing and able to do to make it, the better off you'll be in this world.

"And try not to want stuff all the time," he says. "That helps a lot. People only go into debt when they want stuff they can't afford."

"You have to have a mortgage, Frank. Most people can't afford to buy a house outright."

"Then build it."

I don't say anything right away. On the drive up to Whitney I had listened to a CBC interview with musician Pete Seeger, who told a story of building the only house he had lived in as an adult by buying the land and then the materials when he could afford it. He learned how to build a house by borrowing a book from a New York City public library.

Seeger said not having a mortgage had come in handy over the years. When he wasn't working. Was being blackballed. In jail.

"Is there anything you want that you don't have, Frank?"

"Nothing I can think of."

"What would you buy if you won the lottery?"

"Maybe a twenty-dollar fishing lure."

———◆———

Frank's ideas about money are not that different from the philosophy espoused in the best-selling book *Shop Class as Soulcraft*, by Matthew Crawford.

Crawford had been a fellow at a Virginia think-tank but gave it all up to open a motorcycle repair shop. The book is a paean to physical labour and the trades, advancing the argument that people in North America have become too distant from useful knowledge and useful work.

We can't repair anything in our homes. We need a degree from MIT to change the oil in a car. We have no knowledge or understanding about how most things in our lives work, from smart phones to on-line banking.

As a result we have become a generation of dependent workers. Needing infrastructure and large institutions in order to survive. Always feeling a little stressed over that, unconsciously in most cases, but knowing somewhere deep inside us that if civilization collapsed tomorrow we would be stuck knowing nothing more than search-engine optimization.

Far better off we would have been if we had learned how to fix a motorcycle. Build a house. Pull off a decent spot weld. Knowledge and skills that would help us not only directly but indirectly, give us useful skills by which to make money. Gold bullion. Bit-coins.

Fish equal money. Wood equals money. Frank was making the same argument. Biggest difference was, Frank never had an epiphany and never worked at a think-tank.

So never had the chance to quit a think-tank. Which I'm pretty sure he would have done. If anyone had been smart enough to hire him.

———◆———

Frank needed to talk to his father. A thing easier said than done.

Frank Kuiack Sr. was foreman at the St. Anthony bush-camp on Perieu Lake and was a busy man. He could out-work any man in the camp and so was a good foreman. All anyone had to do was follow his dad around and he would put in a good day's work.

His dad understood work and that was why Frank needed to talk to him.

He had never gone back to the mines. Had cashed in his bus ticket to Timmins two months ago. Had spent the time

LESSON NINE
Twelve Things You Should Eat and Drink

At the age of eighty, Frank Kuiack can still out-portage and out-paddle just about anyone in Algonquin Park. He credits his stamina and strength to daily exercise (though he doesn't call it that) and his diet.

Shown here are the twelve things Frank believes everyone should eat and drink. The Highlands Diet consists of:

1. Fish **3.** Honey **5.** Nescafe instant coffee **7.** Spices
(Secret recipe. You'll need to make your own.)

2. Flour **4.** Trout spread **6.** Cranberry juice

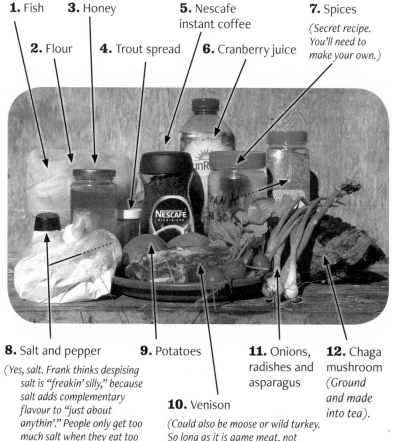

8. Salt and pepper
(Yes, salt. Frank thinks despising salt is "freakin' silly," because salt adds complementary flavour to "just about anythin'." People only get too much salt when they eat too much processed food, he says.)

9. Potatoes

10. Venison
(Could also be moose or wild turkey. So long as it is game meat, not cattle or poultry.)

11. Onions, radishes and asparagus

12. Chaga mushroom *(Ground and made into tea).*

in Cobalt and as much as he had come to love Marie, he had not come to love Cobalt.

He wanted to come home. Wanted Marie and the children to come with him.

But he had no job. So it made no sense, what he was thinking. You needed a job when you were thinking about stuff like that.

Or did you? His father had found a way to live in the Highlands, and he had started with not much more than Frank had right then. Maybe there was a way.

He had to go to Perieu Lake to find him. After waiting at home three days but he never showed. He found his dad by the shore of the lake, watching two men cut down a tree with a mechanical saw.

The saw had a blade on it that must have been more than four feet, a ribbon of blades that ran around the shaft of the saw like the fan belt on a car. One man had to hold the tip of the blade to guide it, being careful not to let the whirring blades cut him, while the second man sliced the blade into the tree.

A mechanical hand-saw. With no carburetor it seemed, for the noise right then was louder than a diesel truck. Frank went and stood beside his father, who said after a few minutes:

"Like t'weren't enough noise here already."

"That's a hell of a racket," agreed Frank.

"Not for long. That t'ing is goin' in the lake tonight. "

He turned to look at his youngest son. No longer a boy but a man in his 20s. Short and tough looking.

"You quit the mines?" he asked.

"Two months ago. I hated it."

His father nodded but didn't say anything.

"I can't work underground dad. I'm just not cut out for it."

"You didn't like ta bush-camp n'ter."

"I know. I don't mind working dad, but I hated those jobs."

"What you like doin' Frankie?"

He thought about it a minute.

"I like being in the bush. I like goin' places in my canoe. I like taking people fishin'"

"All the guides are goin' Frankie. I got Felix Luckasavitch in the camp now."

Frank didn't say anything. Felix Luckasavith was one of the best guides in the Highlands. Every boy in the Luckasavitch family was considered a top guide and two of them had built the main hall at Arowhon Pines Resort.

Just the two of them.

If Felix Luckasavitch wasn't guiding, then Frank really didn't have a plan here. He was just talking.

"I want to move back," he said finally, not knowing what else to say. Down to saying the only thought in his head.

His father turned away from his son to watch the two men working the mechanical saw.

"You wondering what to do Frankie?" he said.

"I am. I want to live here. But I have no job."

His dad turned back to look at him. His son had been a disaster in the bush-camp. If there was even a remote chance of that changing he might have given him different advice.

But there wasn't. And he knew what his son was saying was true. Frankie was a hard worker. He just wasn't made for life in a bush camp.

Before walking over to the two men with the mechanical saw, to explain what would be happening to the saw that night, Frank Kuiack Sr. squeezed his son's shoulder and said:

"Work'll always find ya Frankie. Don'cha worry 'bout t'at. You wanna come home, you should come home."

———◆———

We fish for another hour after lunch, catch two more small bass from another channel, but by two o'clock we are ready to head back to Galeairy Lake.

Frank goes to hide the canoe and I wait by the portage. Some other anglers have appeared on the lake and he is gone longer than usual, no doubt taking pains to hide the boat.

I can't blame him. It was almost normal, a metal Grumman with only a few dents in the bow.

That evening after supper, we go through the guidebook for a few hours and I record some interviews. Before going to bed we watch a television newscast. There is a story about Stephen Harper on an Arctic tour and halfway through the story Frank says:

"I don't miss that at all. If I were going to give anybody advise about politics I'd say run for the hills. Quick!"

That's right. I forgot. I had been fishing that day with a three-term councilor from South Algonquin Township.

———◆———

Politics in the Algonquin Highlands has always been a bit of a blood sport, a rough and tumble, elbows-out affair going back to the late 1800s when Tories and Liberals in Eganville would throw each other off the bridge spanning the Bonnechere River.

The bridge was the de facto dividing line between the Protestant and Catholic sections of the village, which was conveniently also one of the primary distinctions between Whig and Tory.

This was timid stuff, however, compared to the political history of Arnprior, the town at the mouth of the Madawaska River. The town was established — the original governing structure — as the kingdom of a Scottish chieftain.

The chieftain's name was Archibald McNab, 17th hereditary chief of the Clan McNab. He had fled Scotland in the
1820s one step ahead of his creditors. When he arrived
in Upper Canada he petitioned the government for land
along the Madawaska River.

Being a hereditary Scottish chieftain — even a broke and
creditor-fleeing one — had its privileges in the 1820s and
the petition was granted. McNab then brought over more
than one hundred of his clansman and more or less turned
them into chattels.

The government freed the settlers from their legal obli-
gations to McNab some twenty years later, although by this
time he had fled to France, where he died of consumption
after fathering two children and raking up some more bills.

If there is a strain of the slightly off-kilter running through
politics in the Algonquin Highlands, there is a correspond-
ing strain of dogged earnestness. The provincial MLA for
the area is John Yakabuski, former owner of Yakabuski's
Hardware Store in Barry's Bay, a stolid, sleeves-rolled-up
man from whom most people would feel comfortable buying nuts and bolts.

Frank Kuiack, when he ran for public office, was in the
earnest, low-centre-of-gravity political mold of a John Yakabuski. Not a dreamer. Not a bible-thumping evangelist or
Scottish chieftain.

Just someone annoyed that the road to his house never
seemed to get plowed properly. So one spring, after complaining about another bad-plowing season, and being
told by people who had heard it all before that maybe he
should do something about it, he registered to run as a
town councilor, and won.

————◆————

Frank lost the next election by a single vote, and that might
have been the end of his political career except that the

man who beat him died the next year, and as no one in the township had either the memory or desire for a municipal by-election, Frank was asked if he could finish out the term.

He won a third term and that's when the trouble started. That election was for the newly amalgamated township of South Algonquin — five townships put together — and the first item of business was where to locate the new town hall.

None of the existing town halls was considered large or grand enough for a new amalgamated township. Whitney probably had the best one of the lot; a fairly new building not far from the liquor store, although most thought even this would not be grand enough.

As people debated and considered, Frank looked at a map and saw that the village of Madawaska was close to the exact geographic centre of the new township.

So at that first full-council meeting of the newly amalgamated township of South Algonquin, Frank suggested building the new offices in Madawaska. Explaining that was the centre of the new township, and therefore the sensible thing to do.

It is an impossible fact to ascertain (the research for an approximation, an inkling, even a half-decent ballpark guess being insurmountable) but it is quite possible Frank was the first politician in Canada to suggest taking something from his riding and giving it to another riding, because it made sense.

Things did not go well for him.

While councilors from the other former townships thought Frank's suggestion was bold and visionary (not to mention a shorter commute) the councilors from the former township of Airy, where Whitney was located, thought he had lost his mind.

A town clerk who lived in a cottage on Galaiery Lake

Frank casting the deciding vote in the Town Hall Relocation
Debate of 2000

was so incensed at perhaps needing to drive to work that she told people around the village that if she had belonged to a union, she would have filed a grievance against Frank.

A retired McRae Lumber mill-hand who attended every council meeting in Whitney and spoke whenever public presentations were on the agenda (sometimes being surprised when an item was added late to the agenda, but generally being smart enough to form an opinion in time to speak) was just as angry.

Within a few weeks of the clerk and the retired mill-hand doing errands around Whitney, everyone else was just as angry. Only then realizing what an insult this was to their civic pride, moving the town hall to Madawaska.

———◆———

In the run-up to the vote Frank was lobbied by everyone in Whitney, it seemed. The regulars at the Twin E told him they would be some annoyed at having to drive to Madawaska on official town business, which didn't happen all that often, only when their tax bills started arriving with red lettering, but when it did happen they would be some annoyed.

Some business owners talked about recalling Frank, as there should have been a by-election after the last election. Did no one think of that?

The town clerk started to phone him at home, asking if Frank would be giving her rides into work on winter mornings when her car wouldn't start.

When the day of the meeting came Frank was the deciding vote. He didn't back down. He raised his hand and said the town hall should be moved to Madawaska.

It was the end of his political career. He didn't even bother running in the next election, such was the antipathy toward him, and which took some years to abate.

Today, Frank says he was right about Madawaska being the logical choice for the new town hall, but maybe wrong about everything else. When so many people are telling you you're wrong, you should probably listen to them. Especially when they're your neighbours.

Other than that, he doesn't say much about the Great Relocation Debate, other than to offer the opinion: "A lot of it could have been avoided if people had just looked at a map."

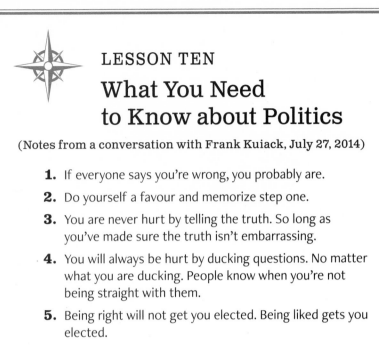

LESSON TEN
What You Need to Know about Politics

(Notes from a conversation with Frank Kuiack, July 27, 2014)

1. If everyone says you're wrong, you probably are.

2. Do yourself a favour and memorize step one.

3. You are never hurt by telling the truth. So long as you've made sure the truth isn't embarrassing.

4. You will always be hurt by ducking questions. No matter what you are ducking. People know when you're not being straight with them.

5. Being right will not get you elected. Being liked gets you elected.

6. This is not as bad as it seems because unpopular people are well known for making bad decisions (in facial hair, hygiene, general temperament) but popular people tend to make good decisions (work for money, take care of children, have a skill).

7. Because the above two steps are so important, if you are interested in becoming a politician ask this question: Do people like me? If no, become a dentist.

8. If you want to run for public office because of some grand idea, the righting of wrongs, the yelling of "The emperor has no clothes," the riding of white horses, slaying of dragons and anything else that makes you feel good about yourself and being around other people, stop and ask yourself this question: Do people like me? If no, become a journalist.

9. Never get discouraged by what you are doing. Public service remains important and worthwhile work. It only looks absurd most days.

10. Be sincere.

11. Work hard.

12. Never look at maps.

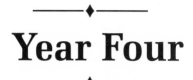

Year Four

Never say goodbye because goodbye means going away and going away means forgetting.

— J.M. Barrie, *Peter Pan*

Many fish bite
If you got good bait

— "Fishin' Blues,"
traditional, first recorded by Henry Thomas, 1928

♦ 8 ♦

Another bad winter — Frank has a health scare — Climbing trees — Marie goes to a nursing home — A small gift

The winter of 2014-2015 was another long one for most of Canada. Toronto had its coldest February since weather recording started back in 1840. Montreal went forty-seven days without having a day above zero degrees Celsius. Ottawa had a string of thirty-nine days that never went above freezing.

The Maritimes had record cold plus record snowfalls, including a string of thirty-centimetre-plus snowfalls in late February and March that shut down Halifax for days, along with most of the North-Eastern Seaboard.

It became a craze in Boston to film people jumping off their roofs into snow-banks.

The Prairies did not have as much snow as central Canada, but shivered through another cold winter. Cold-temperature records were set in much of Alberta. Winnipeg again had week after week that never went above freezing.

And in Saskatchewan — which had been the epi-centre of cold weather for four years running — a caller to a Saskatoon talk show one February morning probably spoke for an entire province when he asked the host if she was serious, when she had called it "another glorious morning," or was she saying that: "just to keep people from offing themselves?"

———◆———

Frank lost his brother that winter. Edmund was the last brother Frank had and he supposes he should be grateful for that. The brother he was closest to was the last one.

Dominique was long gone. Maxie was gone. Ambrose had been gone for decades, drowned during a log run down the Petawawa River, his body not found for eight days. Just like Tom Thomson's body. Eight days seemed to be the norm for drowned men.

Edmund used to be cheek and jowl with Frank during the drinking years, a good brother after that when Frank quit, not standoffish the way some people around Whitney became.

Edmund cared not a whit that Frank quit drinking. Wasn't going to slow him any.

Edmund could go through a 40-ounce bottle of rye while sitting in his ice-fishing hut for an afternoon. Then go out drinking that night. His wife was a good woman who rarely drank, never smoked, and yet Lorraine had passed away before Edmund. Her death rattled Edmund and he quit drinking shortly afterwards.

Edmund could have drunk all day if he wanted, now that he was on his own. Many widows and widowers do exactly that. But all it took for Edmund to quit was a few mornings waking up alone, hung over and feeling the way men in their 60s feel when they wake up hung over—which is a special kind of hurt — and that was enough to make him quit.

There was now a sad loneliness to drinking and it would never be any different. Edmund was smart enough to know that.

So he quit drinking and started going to AA meetings with Frank. You could never say Edmund was in good shape, but before long he had lost twenty pounds and also his river-gravel skin complexion, which until then everyone had assumed was natural.

A few weeks after Christmas Edmund got the flu, which turned into pneumonia, and so he was taken to hospital. One morning, bored out of his gourd, Edmund got up and tried to open a window. He fell on the way and broke his hip.

The next week he died on an operating table while doctors tried to repair the hip. Edmund Kuiack was seventy eight.

"Stupid way to die," Frank said, during one of our winter phone conversations. "Who'd ever think a hospital'd be the thing to kill ya."

———◆———

Frank phoned me a few times that spring to ask how the guidebook was going, and when I might be coming up. When I left Whitney the previous year I thought the book would be completed by early autumn. Had said as much.

Might have happened, too, if I had come back to Ottawa and started working on it. Instead, I came back and got busy. A municipal election was underway in the nation's capital and I was asked by the Ottawa Sun to write an extra column, just on the election.

The radio show was in a ratings period. Football camp started for William. Hailey was working her first part-time job and her father was providing transportation.

Although I never told Frank, I didn't look at the *Last Guide's Guide* for months when I returned from our bass fishing trip. I wanted to work on it. Would have liked to work on it. I was just too busy doing everything that needed to be done.

It struck me as something revelatory the previous summer, discovering the difference between the things you like to do, and the things you need to do. It was no less a revelation one year later, when I saw how easy it was to forget it.

———◆———

One day in early June my daughter came into my study and found me working on the guidebook. Frank had phoned the week before and we were going to go fishing the following month.

I wasn't sure how I was going to find the time to do that, but I had to tell Frank something when he asked about the book. That's what I came up with. Let's go fishing.

Now I was going through the transcribed interviews and notes, the rough chapters and lessons, wondering if I could get it finished in time. Knowing already that I couldn't. And I must have been looking worried about that because Hailey said:

"It doesn't look like you're having fun, Dad."

"Don't think I am."

"That's Frank's book you're working on?"

"Yes."

"Shouldn't that be fun?"

"It should be. No, it is. It's just been going on a little too long. I need to finish it and give it to him."

"Frank liked his first book a lot."

"I know he did. That book changed a lot of things for him."

"Is Frank like your dad?"

"What? No, what makes you say that?"

"Are you sure? You seem to like him an awful lot."

———◆———

The first, unexpected phone call Frank received after *The Last Guide* was published came from Whitney Elementary School, asking if he could come and read to a class of students. Perhaps sign a few books while he was there.

Frank wasn't sure what to make of the call. He and Marie had lived within a few blocks of the school for decades but never been inside. It was not the school Frank had attended as a boy and he had no fond memories of the school.

In the principal's office a teacher was waiting for him, a young man who shook his hand and said it was a pleasure to meet him.

The man then led him to a small classroom, saying as they walked that he had been reading Frank's story to his children, a grade three class, for the past two weeks.

When they entered the classroom Frank saw a wall of crayon drawings, each one showing — in different colours, with different levels of skill — an old man fishing from a boat.

"That's you," a young boy said when he ran up to Frank and Frank said it was a good likeness, could tell it was him a mile away.

After that came calls from people wanting to hire him as a fishing guide. Magazines in the United States phoned, asking if Frank could take their photographers around. The Discovery Channel phoned asking the same thing. As did the Ontario government.

The phone calls from people who said they had read the Last Guide and stopped drinking came later. He's not sure why that would be. Although he remembered how hard it had been to quit, so maybe it was nothing more than that. Some things took more time.

In late June Frank phoned to cancel our fishing trip.

"What's come up?" I asked, trying not to sound too relieved.

"I can't walk."

"You can't walk?"

"Can't walk good. My feet and ankles are killin' me. Pain is shooting up my leg. No way I could do a portage right now."

"Have you been to a doctor?"

"Going later this week."

"The boy doctor?"

"He's a bit older now, but yeah, him. He's not so bad, I guess. He likes fishin'. I wouldn't have thought that the first time I met him."

"My Lord, Frank, I'm sorry to hear this."

"Yeah, I thought it would go away. But I've used up all the Chinese liniment I got, wrapped my feet in tenser bandages, taken all sorts of baths, but nothin's working. I think it might be a nerve or somethin'."

"Are you able to get around at all?"

"Oh yeah. I can drive all right. When there's no pressure on the foot it's fine."

"What about when you're walking?"

"Got a cane."

"You're using a cane?"

"Just when I'm up."

———◆———

It was easy to discount Frank's health scares. They had been so many, varied, and in one or two instances memorable, it was almost natural to assume he would always come out the other side, if not unscathed, then certainly laughing at what had happened and ready to move on.

His worst health scare had probably been the bad eye, three years earlier. Or at least that was the only one that truly seemed to worry him.

In 1965 Frank was changing a tire in front of the Algonquin Lunch Bar, a rimless tire, which they don't make anymore, for exactly what happened to Frank. The tire exploded and pressurized air and rubber hit him in the chest with the force of a pneumatic jackhammer.

He was in hospital six months, wearing a full upper-body cast for most of that time. When he was released his hands

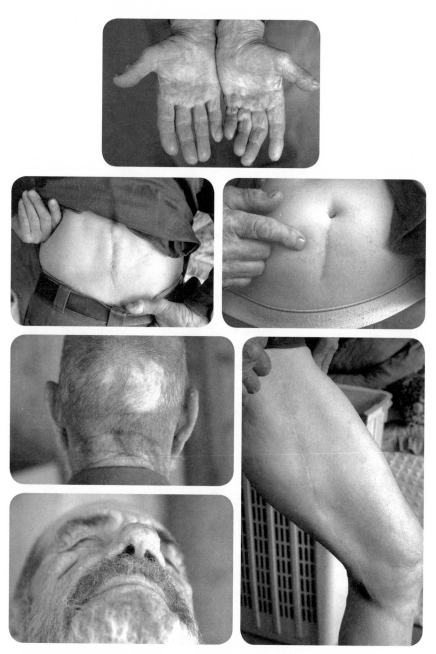

A compilation of Frank's most notable scars, including leg grafts, surgical lines, nose tumours and a steel plate in his head

were still in casts, so he couldn't roll cigarettes.

Marie took advantage of the situation by installing a "Thank You for Not Smoking" sign in the middle of the living room, thinking if Frank couldn't smoke, and couldn't see anyone smoking, he would quit.

But that didn't happen. Instead, Frank took to sneaking cigarettes behind his work shed, getting friends to roll his cigarettes and hold them up to his lips. He'd ask people to drop by and do that for him. Marie was pleased to see Frank had so many friends who cared enough about him to visit often.

Another time, he was coming out of Source Lake, carrying the hind quarters of a moose strapped to his back. He had been guiding a hunting party and the moose they shot that day was huge. Wanting to show off, Frank field-dressed the animal and then strapped on the back half. Started hiking out. Ran a few times because he liked hearing people behind him scream, "Do you see what he's doing now?"

Then he was running downhill and that was his mistake. Either that or being drunk. Probably a combination of the two. But he was running downhill and he tripped and the moose meat twisted on him, ripping muscles and nerves right off his spine.

He heard it peel off. A sound he'll never forget. Like Velcro. Only it came from inside him.

The hunting party carried him out on a stretcher fashioned from birch trees and drove straight to the Peterborough Hospital. He had surgery that same night.

Over his life Frank has also: lost a kidney; broken both hands, both arms and both legs; had an artificial vein put in his left leg; two stints put in his right leg; eye surgery twice to remove cysts; a metal plate put into his skull (after the rimless tire accident); surgery to remove calluses on both hands; surgery to remove calluses on both feet; a broken collar bone; broken ribs; and perhaps the ultimate wonky health ailment: surgery to remove a benign tumour on the end of his nose.

Frank has such a marvelous nose, a textured and omnipresent thing of beauty, after the surgery only a few people noticed the nose was now shorter.

So he's had a whole lot of ailments and bust-ups and although common sense will tell you there has to be an end-game one day — some sort of health problem will eventually retire him — it's always been easy to believe that day was far away.

Now, even as he talked about his bad leg, I remained relieved that Frank was cancelling our fishing trip. I was so locked into work-mode I didn't even feel shame for what I was about to do. Use Frank's bad leg as the excuse for not finishing the book.

The problem with my plan was — Frank kept talking.

"If the doctor can fix my legs I'll probably do most of my guiding out of Arowhon this summer."

"They like you down there, Frank."

"They seem to. Theresa says I could have customers 'prit near every day if I wanted. It's really coming back, fishin' in the Park."

"It's worked out pretty well for you."

"I suppose. May have to take a couple days off in September tho'. Adele is talking about coming up."

"During trout season?"

"Yep."

"I thought you had a rule about not taking time off during trout season."

"Normally do. But this year'll be different I guess."

"Why?"

"You don't 'member? I'm turnin' eighty this year, Ron."

———◆———

The guilt came in waves after that.

That's right. Frank's birthday was September 16th. He was turning eighty. I knew that.

I had just forgotten.

"I'm going to come up anyway, Frank," I heard myself say. "You need to take a look at this guidebook. It's just about done."

"Right on"

———◆———

The end of July I was driving back to Whitney, a lawyer's box on the backseat of my Jeep with the words Last Guide's Guide written on it. Inside were maps, rough drafts of chapters and lessons, photographs, books and anything else I had collected over the past three years, from matchbook covers to a small, cardboard Canadian flag Drago Dumancic had given me on the shores of Rock Lake.

It felt good to be back in the Highlands and by the time I had driven through Eganville I was asking myself what had taken so long. I stopped for lunch at the Wilno Tavern, getting a seat by the window, where I watched smoke rising from the hills, coming from the chimneys of homes I couldn't see.

In Barry's Bay I stopped for gas and watched a man push a lawnmower down the sidewalk, pull up to the pump next to mine, and put in fifteen cents' worth of gas. I stood beside him at the cash register, as he handed over a quarter and waited for change.

For most of the drive I listened to a Hank Williams CD I had recently purchased. It had a radio interview and two live performances recorded in 1952.

Williams talked after every song. Jokes about making "a whole lot of beans" on this next song, or another song being "popular right across the country, on the pop charts, the folk charts, the hillbilly charts, you name it and it was there!" (The song was *Your Cold, Cold Heart*.)

He boasted often, told jokes when he wasn't boasting, spoke in clipped consonants with syllables sometimes dropped at the end or beginning of words, crazy spiking inflections on other words. It was a form of speech you might have called folksy, or down-home and I couldn't decide if it was partially put on. It was the sort of speaking that would have been expected from the Hillbilly Shakespeare.

It also sounded familiar. Halfway through the radio interview Williams was asked about some of the clubs he used to play in Alabama, the interviewer reading a list of names that just cracked him up. When the list was finished Williams said:

"I sure do 'member. Holy Jeepers."

———◆———

When I got to Frank's house he showed me his cane, more a walking stick really, with an ornate handle that looked like bone, engravings of wolves and spruce hills etched into the bone.

"You pick this out?" I asked.

"I did."

"Looks like a medicine stick or something."

"Thing's heavy as all get-out. 'Magine being hit in the head with it."

All right. Not a medicine stick.

We had a light supper, baked beans and fried eggs, toast we lathered with trout jam. Frank pulled out *The Canoe Routes of Algonquin Park* map and we started examining it. Frank used a washable yellow highlighter to circle lakes he thought we might try. Which was something new. In the past he had simply pointed at the lakes. He seemed tired that night as well, which was something he normally hid.

"Foot still bothering you?"

"A little. Not much."

"Surgery was two weeks ago?"

"That's right."

"Another blocked artery?"

"That's what it was. Got two stints in there now."

"Would something be causing that to happen all the time?"

"Probably," and then he laughed, told me what had happened at his doctor's appointment. It was with the boy-doctor and shortly into the examination he told Frank there was another blocked artery in his leg. Just like his other leg had been blocked a few years ago. Not as bad this time. They weren't going to need a graft.

"But something is causing this to happen, Frank. What do you do in a day?"

"What do I do?"

"Yes, tell me your daily activities."

Well, not an easy question, but Frank did as best he could. Chopping wood, fishing, canoeing, gardening, carpentry and maintenance work around the house, some of that at Arowhon too, bow-hunting in the fall, some ice-fishing, not so much anymore, cook, clean, put out the garbage, catch minnows.

"None of that sounds like a problem," said the doctor. "There's pressure on the artery somehow. Probably coming from your feet."

"My feet?"

"Almost certainly. There's really no way for the blockage to start in the upper body. Can you think of anything else, Frank?"

The boy-doctor looked at him expectantly, and with such an earnest and guileless expression Frank went searching far back in his memory, looking for something to offer the boy, until finally he said:

"I take down trees sometimes."

"Take down trees? What do you mean, Frank?"

"I take down trees. The school in Bancroft had a bunch for me last year. Other people phone me up."

"Take it down, like a lumberjack?"

"Yeah, like that."

"I saw someone do that at the Pembroke Fair. You climb up the tree, with a chainsaw on your back? You have a belt around your waist and you cinch yourself up?"

"That's right."

"You have spurs on your feet, to get a good grip on the wood. You stick them in and you climb up the tree?"

"Yeah, they're like cowboy spurs, only made special for climbin' trees. You can put 'em on your work boots and ... Hey, do you think that might have somethin' to do with it?"

The doctor said to stop climbing trees. Frank said all right. Although he tried it last week and said there wasn't a problem. So long as he tied a rope to the chainsaw and pulled it up by hand once he was in position in the tree.

"Long as there's no weight on my back when I'm climbin' it's OK."

I didn't argue. Kept looking at the map.

"You sure you're up for this?"

"Oh yeah. Already been guiding twice this week. What do you want to go after?"

"I was thinking about lake trout."

"Thought you'd say that," and Frank started to fold the map. "We'll go back to Head Lake. They've been biting good in there this year."

———◆———

That night I slept in the spare bedroom Frank's wife used, when he was away on lengthy fishing trips. Marie had trouble sleeping in their bed when Frank wasn't in it. Some part of her subconscious knew something was missing and threw off her sleep. She had no problems in another bed.

Her sewing machine was still in the corner of the room. Her clothes in the closet. Her magazines on the nightstand, one with a page still turned down.

Marie had died ten years earlier. On a fishing trip not long afterwards, Frank told me that the hardest thing he'd ever had to do was put his wife in a home. He had fought hard to avoid it. Would have liked her to spend her last days in Whitney, in the home they had lived in for nearly forty years.

He quit overnight guiding to try and make that happen. Hired a woman from Portugal to help with the chores. It was harder than he expected. Marie always ate like a bird and soon it was a struggle to get her to eat anything. She couldn't manage the stairs and Frank carried her outside most days, as it was easier that way.

She seemed unaware of her surroundings a lot of the time and that was hard as well. Frank never knew when the woman he had known and loved since he was a young man would suddenly look at him with fear in her eyes, not recognizing him and wondering why he was sitting so close.

Still, he could have handled all that. It was her heart attack that made it impossible. After that happened, her doctor said there was no way she could stay in Whitney. She needed round-the-clock medical care.

"You just can't do it, Frank," the doctor told him. "It's not a matter of will."

Frank, who believes most things in life are a matter of will, refused to accept it. He fought with the doctor. Fought with his children. In the end it was Marie who finally told him she should go. The doctor was right.

———◆———

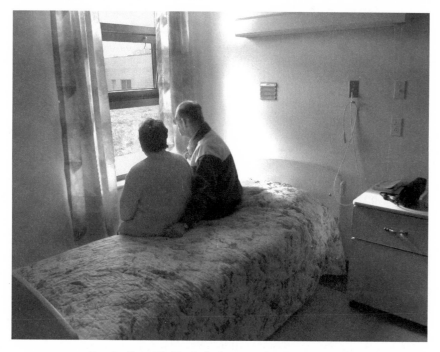

Frank sits with Marie in her nursing-home room

They chose a nursing home in Cornwall, where Marie would be close to their daughter Adele and her family. Frank drove down the second week of January, the day clear and unseasonably warm. Just the two of them. The heater was turned on in the van, but running so low you could barely hear it.

"Nice day," said Marie and Frank, not knowing how to respond, not feeling it was a nice day at all, said nothing. Later in the trip they talked about chores that would need to be done around the house when spring came. Neither was confused by the weather. They were talking about chores to be done weeks away. A half-hour outside Ottawa, Marie fell asleep and didn't awaken until they reached the home.

Frank wheeled her to her room, insisting on doing that, then arranged her clothes and belongings, stayed until the sun had gone and she had fallen asleep again. After that he walked quietly out the room, went to his van, rummaged around a cooler in the back, and returned to the home.

He found the charge-nurse and gave her the three packages wrapped in butcher's paper he had taken from the cooler. Told her there were fish inside. Trout. If Marie could have one for supper tomorrow she would be happy. The other two were for the nurse. A small gift.

Marie had one more heart attack and nine minor strokes in the Cornwall home before she passed away the following year. The first few strokes were not noticed, but the last were all verified by CAT scans. Her brain misfiring, synapses surging and sending out electric shocks, tiny black holes left behind when her brain snapped back on line. Light gone dark. Energy vanished. Right in her mind. You could see it in the pictures.

How she lived through that no doctor was quite sure. One or two strokes, maybe. But nine? It was so far on the outer reaches of possible that most doctors saw it as the sort of thing you ran across from time to time, a thing unexplained, a crack in medical knowledge, and you either had to accept what had happened or drive yourself insane looking for an answer that would never come.

She was hanging on for some reason. That was all there was to it.

The last three strokes happened within two weeks of each other, at the endt of March, and Frank went to the home to see her. Stayed two days. Sitting beside her bed for most of that time, holding her hands, reading to her, even though there was no sign that Marie knew he was there.

When he drove home, on the morning of the third day, the sun sat higher in the sky than it had for months and the Ottawa River was open the whole way. There were buds on some of the trees and just south of Ottawa he saw some robins.

Marie passed away the next day. With her passing the doctors in the home came to believe she had been hanging on to see Frank. Which might have been possible. Frank thought it might have been possible.

He also thought it possible she was doing exactly what he would be doing when the time came, if he had been lying in that bed.

Trying to make sure he made it to the end of winter. So he wouldn't be leaving mid-season. With the feeling things had been left unresolved.

Marie and Frank

LESSON ELEVEN
How to Fall in Love

"I met Marie on a bus going to Cochrane; noticed her the moment I got on (She was) sittin' by herself. She always claimed to be five feet, but she was under that. She was this growed-up kid sittin' on the bus all by herself.

"Gettin' together with Marie was 'bout the easiest thing I ever done. No harder'n fallin' down.

"I loved my first wife all right, and if she hadn't walked out on me we would have stayed together. But it weren't the right time for us.

"Maybe you could say I didn't love her enough to quit drinking, so it wasn't real love, and maybe you'd be right. I don't know. It hurt like something real when she left.

"(I remember that) everything was beautiful the year (Marie) moved in with me. Sun every day. Pine needles on the ground lit up like coals or something whenever you went for a hike. Everything seemed so good when Marie moved in.

"Maybe that's part of it. Why it lasted so long for us. Lovin' someone is maybe just part of what you need. ...maybe the rest is feelin' that way 'bout everythin' else too."

◆9◆

Going back to Head Lake — The funny thing about fishing — Finding Frank in a photograph — A good age

Frank's alarm goes off at 4:30 a.m. I lie in bed and smile.

I get dressed and go to to the darkened kitchen, where he is already sitting with a cup of coffee.

"You made that pretty quickly," I say.

"Couldn't sleep. Got up early. The kettle's still hot."

I make a cup of coffee and sit with him. Neither of us speak as we eat our breakfast: frosted flakes; white toast; sliced tomatoes from his garden. We wash up and when I walk out of the bathroom he is already walking down the stairs with the backpacks and fishing rods.

"Ready to go?" he yells. I watch his back disappear through the basement door. I'd better be ready to go. I knew Frank well enough to know we had talked about his bad leg too much last night, in his opinion, and he was making a point of showing me it wasn't going to slow him down any.

The Algonquin Highlands may never have offered people much. By way of land and an easy go of it. But if you could live here, it offered pride by the bucket-load.

———◆———

We drive through Whitney and then through Algonquin Park, not the only car on the road this time of year. We pass a couple of pickup trucks with what look to be other early-morning anglers. A Volkswagen Microbus with Illinois plates. An Opeongo Outfitters truck, stacked with canoes, on its way to drop off boats at campsites in the Park.

We make the turn into the Cache Lake boat-launch and a few minutes later are on the water, the lights of Bartlett Lodge, built on an island in the lake, guiding us down the lake in the near darkness of early dawn,

The mist has not yet started to burn off the lake and there are times when it is thick enough to swirl over the gunnels of the boat. We hear birds singing out from the shoreline. Hear something splashing in the lake. Probably beavers, although we can't see anything.

At the portage we beach the boat and start the long walk into Head Lake. The mist is thick in the valleys of the forest as well and we hike through what look like clouds driven to the ground. At the end of the portage the sun is clearing the tree-line of the lake. We can faintly hear the waterfalls coming down from Kenneth Lake, at the far end of the lake.

Twenty minutes later we are sitting in Frank's rotten-lettuce green canoe, cork-handled trolling rods in our hands, Penn reels with steel line letting out Williams Wablers.

———◆———

We start trolling past the western shore of Head Lake, working a deep channel of water. Frank has said to run the lure at thirty feet. He paddles and trolls and looks at his fish finder while doing all that. Sometimes he will roll a cigarette.

Head Lake is a favourite of Franks. It is not only where *The Last Guide's Guide* began, but also where he took me eight years ago, when I came to Whitney looking for his advice. My wife had suggested it. "Go talk to Frank."

We sat in his canoe that day and I talked about all the changes happening at the *Ottawa Citizen*. The newspaper was about to kill its Sunday magazine. Where Frank's story had first appeared. Long form journalism was dying, or already dead, and where would that leave me?

I had hashed out the problem with friends and colleagues in Ottawa for several weeks. Had every shape and manner of answer given to me, from ride it out at the newspaper to become a hedge-fund manager in New York City, as a group of them were about to buy the *Citizen*. Maybe that's how you get to set editorial policy.

Clever advice. Just didn't help much.

So I went to see Frank. I had already come to see Frank as one of the happiest and contended people I knew, and as I was neither right then, maybe he had something to say.

I went through the problem with him, the dilemma it had left me, the possible solutions to the problem, the possible "up-side and down-side" to each possible solution. I talked and talked.

When I had run out of things to say Frank said:

"So you wanna write?"

"Yes, that's what I've been saying."

"Well then, write."

He shrugged his shoulders and didn't say anything else. Kept paddling the canoe around Head Lake. The answer was there if I wanted it. Up to me.

The bemused expression on his face for the next few minutes is what I imagined the expression on Basil Sawyer's face had been the day he twisted Bud Williams fishing lure and gave it back to him.

What, you want me to do all the work for you Sport?

Two days after the fishing trip, I quit the *Citizen*.

———◆———

Once again we have no luck trolling down the western shore of Head Lake. Once again Frank is surprised.

"The fish finder is showing lakers at 30 feet," he says. "We should have had some strikes by now."

He taps the fish-finder. Maybe it's lying.

"Are you sure it's lakers?"

"At thirty feet, a school that size, it's got to be lakers. Ain't nothin' else it can be."

I'm not that worried. I enjoy trolling, with or without fish. The Penn reel I am using has a solid weight to it. Feels good in my hands as I jerk the rod back and forth. I let out line from time to time. Reel it back in. For something to do mostly, although I like the sound of the steel line pooling around the spool, the line-guide moving back and forth; the metal components clicking and clacking.

The rod is stiff bamboo with brass eyelets and thick cork handle, worn down slightly in the middle so there is a groove for your hand to slide into. What I'm holding in my hands should last a hundred years if I treat it right.

Frank is now slapping the fish finder.

"It's got to be lyin'. No freakin' way we pass over a school of lakers for two hours and get nothin'."

"Didn't you tell me once that fishing was the one thing you can learn how to do, and it doesn't matter how good you get, you can always go out and be a complete failure?"

"May have said something like that."

"I thought about it later and you're right. Just about everything we do, if you learn how to do it well, you expect a certain result. A marathoner runner isn't going to hit a brick wall at ten feet. A musician isn't going to go tone deaf on stage."

"Don't know if I thought about it that much."

"But you're right. A fisherman can fail any time he goes out. Complete failure."

"Little early in the day to be talkin' like that."

"It's interesting. That's all I'm saying."

"If the dang fish finder was workin'."

"Complete failures. You and me."

"Can ya shaddup. I'm tryin' to concentrate."

———◆———

Be prepared to fail is advice Frank gives every client before heading out, just to make sure they understand.

You may not think he would need to do that, but you'd be surprised. He's had people book him and halfway through the day ask where the salmon are hiding. He's read about people contacting expedition companies in Nepal and asking what sort of shops are on top of Mount Everest.

So he makes sure that people understand. We might not catch fish. No guarantees in this world.

Maybe it isn't as strange as it first seems, when you stretch it out a little, if you assume the other person in the canoe knows nothing at all about fishing.

Because you do expect a certain result, when you've done something for a long time, when you've practiced it and become about as good as possible at doing that certain thing. Frank saw a man on a talk show one day, who said you could learn anything in the world after ten thousand hours of practice. Which struck Frank as true. That you could do such a thing.

Problem with fishing is, no matter how good you become, you can go out tomorrow and get the same result as a one-day rookie. You can be as confident about your abilities as it is possible to become, yet fail. Have every reasonable right and expectation to win, yet lose.

Frank has no idea why fishing is the one thing we do that most closely resembles life. Just knows that it does.

———◆———

We stay trolling on the western shore for most of the morning. Don't move to the middle channel, or the deep pools at the far end of the lake by the waterfalls. The fish finder is showing a school of lakers and Frank is going to stay until he can figure out what the problem is.

There are fishermen trolling the middle of the lake and one caught a nice laker twenty minutes ago. Maybe ten pounds said Frank, who took out his field glasses to have a look at the fish in the net.

But he's not moving. Not going to start acting like some tournament bass fisherman, flitting across the lake. The fish are here. Just need to get their attention somehow.

Shortly after ten a.m. the sun rises to about two feet above the tree-line and a band of sunlight drops onto the surface of the lake. A perfect ribbon of light that was not there two minutes ago, now stretches east to west down Head Lake. On pretty much the exact course we have been trolling.

Within a minute I get a strike. A solid whomp in my arm and when I pull back on the rod I can feel weight at the other end. The rod starts to bend and twitch.

"Did ya see that?" yells Frank. "The sun is hittin' the lure different. You've got the gold Wabler?"

"That's right."

"I'm changin' mine up."

It wasn't a big fish but Frank whooped like a young boy when it was brought into the boat. A two-pound laker. Nice vee-shaped tail. Good green-grey colouring on the flanks. Frank kept whooping and laughing, switching his lure out, saying a few times what a great fish it was.

Which it wasn't. Although it did have the distinction of being the first fish of the day.

So that bit of advice he had earlier? Forget about it.

———◆———

We catch four more lakers in the next forty-five minutes, release each one except for a three-and-a-half pounder that Frank catches. We troll down the path the sun has given us, letting out line, setting the lure at trout depth; getting a strike on each pass.

Once I get a strike while letting out my line, something that happens so rarely it is worth talking about.

"What depth were you at when it hit?"

"Twenty maybe?"

"They're loving that gold Wabler."

"They really are."

"The big ones must be underneath. They're feeding like crazy if they're hitting the lure as it's droppin'. We need to go deeper."

"Have you ever thought about using a down-rigger?"

"Maybe when I'm dead. I'll slow the canoe so you can get it down quicker."

An hour later the sky clouds over, we lose the sun, and we don't stick with it more than fifteen minutes before going for our shore lunch.

———◆———

We go to the campsite by the waterfalls coming out of Kenneth Lake, where we have had a shore lunch before, and I watch Frank go to work. He has the fire burning in two minutes, all the wood he will need gathered and placed by the hearth. Goes to the shoreline to begin filleting the lake trout.

He hasn't slowed much since I've been watching him do this. Hobbles a bit now while he works, which is a strange thing to witness, a fast hobble, but he's still about as quick. One thing that hasn't changed in fifteen years.

A lot of other things changed for him. After the publication of *The Last Guide* Frank began to get phone calls from people who had read the book. Anglers in southern Ontario who wanted to hire him. People who wanted to tell him they had quite drinking after reading his story, and thank you.

From once being the town drunk, a person you crossed the street to avoid if you saw him after two p.m., Frank had morphed into one of Whitney's favourite sons. The author Roy MacGregor, whose family once lived in Whitney, read

Frank cleaning fish for a shore lunch

The Last Guide and wrote in a back-page blurb for the re-issue that frank's story would "feed your soul forever."

Michael Budman, co-founder of Roots (a company inspired by Budman and partner Don Green's love of Algonquin Park) tracked him down and hired him as a regular guide for guests at his cottage on Canoe Lake. Frank has since gone fishing with Michael Douglas. Catherine Zeta Jones. Jeff Bridges.

A lot of strange things to happen to a man in his seventh decade. The American poet Robert Frost once said that all he had learned about life could be summed up in three words. It goes on.

———◆———

The cooked trout, as always, is wonderful. Frank serves it with sliced tomatoes and baked beans, cooked right in the can atop the fire. Frank shows off like he did the first time I saw him cook beans that way, by reaching over the fire and grabbing the tin with his hands. Scooping the beans onto my plate. Taking his time about it.

"You ever wonder if that's why you get calluses, Frank?"

"Nah, it's why I get burns."

———◆———

We go back to fishing and have no luck for the first hour, but then the sky clears, the sun comes back, and another band of light appears on the surface of Head Lake. We paddle toward it and after Frank has checked the depth on his fish finder, we begin trolling.

Frank has a nice laker on his line within five minutes. I catch one shortly afterward and then it is just goofy, how easy it becomes. We catch fish after fish. Paddling down that band of light. On not a single pass do we turn around at the end empty-handed.

It goes on for ninety minutes and it was ninety minutes only because we finally had to stop and leave. Some of the best fishing I've had in Algonquin Park since I was a boy, fishing Ryan Lake with my father, when they used to stock that lake with rainbow trout.

"Gawd, that's a nice fish," Frank says whenever a trout is brought into the boat.

"The tail looks a little off," I might say, and Frank would answer:

"Got a bit of speckle in it, but it's still a laker. Ain't no dots. See that?"

I'd see that. We release the fish. Catch another. It doesn't occur to us, right then, that it could be any other way.

———◆———

We start the hike home shortly after three, both of us with our limit of trout in our backpacks. Near the end of the hike, as we approach the portage to Cache Lake, I hang back a little, so I can see Frank cut through the forest.

One of my favourite photos of Frank was taken on the portage into Ragged Lake. It was taken from behind, from a distance, so you see him surrounded by soaring white pine, old growth pine, the giants of the forest that the lumber companies missed a century ago, and he was almost lost in the frame.

The photo appeared in *The Last Guide* and some have told me, over the years, that it made them sad, to see that photo. Said Frank looked small and frail, "almost inconsequential" is how one person described it to me. And this upset him somehow, to know that even a person like Frank was destined to walk through this thing we call nature with no more worth, import or prominence in a photo than a tree root or a Chaga mushroom.

I always loved the photo. Loved the way Frank wasn't easy to find right away. The way he blended in, and how you could tell, once you found him, that he was walking crooked, leaning toward the path ahead, a bred-in-the-bones Highlands way of walking you see all over Whitney;

Frank hiking through the woods

a way of walking so if you ever trip or stumble, you fall forward. ("There's no sense falling backwards, son. No sense
in a thing like that at all.")

I never saw Frank as inconsequential in that photo. I saw
him as someone who was just there. Belonging more perfectly in the frame than if it had been a portrait.

That night as I sit at Frank's kitchen table we go through
the guidebook. He looks at the photos and says he thinks
he doesn't look bad in a bathing suit, for a seventy-nine-
year-old man. What do I think?

He reads some of the chapters. The lessons. Says there
isn't enough in there about fishing.

"You have to be kidding me."

"No. You got the stories all right. But you need more. Do
you have the most important thing about fishing? That you
gotta know where the fish are?"

"That's in there."

"And tournament bass fishermen? Have we made fun of
them anywhere?"

"I'm pretty sure we have."

"Zipping all over the lake like a dog in heat. Freakin'
annoying."

"I'll make sure it's there."

"I'd 'preciate that."

That night, before going to bed, as we sit at Frank's kitchen
table watching a television newscast, I ask him one last
question:

"Do you wonder how long you're going to be able to keep
guiding?"

I'd never actually asked him the question. Four years
down the road, it occurs to me I probably should.

As he has done throughout the interviews, Frank takes his time before answering. He normally answers in short sentences, with long pauses between the sentences. He often runs his hands over his head during the pauses, beneath his ball-cap, lifting the cap and scratching his head, sliding the cap back on his head.

Sometimes he sighs. Says Jeepers. Then he'll give me another sentence.

Sometimes he comes back later in the day, to add one more.

"My dad lived to be ninety-eight," he says. "My granddad to one hundred and five. I figure I got a few good years left."

We don't say anything for a minute. Sit at Frank's kitchen table drinking our Nescafe coffee, Frank smoking what he has said will be his last cigarette of the night.

Just as I'm wondering if I should rinse my cup and go to bed, he says:

"I think ya got the wrong way of looking at it. It's not 'bout what you won't be able to do anymore; it's 'bout what you've already done. I like being this old. I know what works and what don't. I know what I like, and what I don't. It's a good age."

I don't say anything right away. Don't now whether I should. Frank seems to sense the question I am likely not going to ask and as he rises to go to bed, says:

"Do you like autumn?"

"I do. It's my favourite season."

"Really? Why would that be? Don't autumn mean the year's 'most over?"

"Well sure, but ... "

I sit there for a few seconds wondering what I want to say next. In that time Frank, perhaps realizing this won't be quick, goes to bed.

$\cdot$ 10 $\cdot$

Getting lost on the way to Whitney — A surprise birthday party — We've been waiting a long time — A special dinner at Arowhon Pines Resort

Frank had two birthday parties when he turned eighty. The first took place the weekend before his actual birthday, a surprise party organized by his family.

Sons and daughters, grandchildren and great-grand-children; one great-great-granddaughter, came to Whitney from Cornwall, Peterborough, Ottawa and Nord du Nord in Quebec (where Marie was from.) A caravan of RVs and campers and pick-up trucks had to be hidden for a day, so Frank wouldn't see anyone.

No place in Whitney was large enough and so they all drove to a group campsite on Whitefish Lake, where they spent the Friday night before the party.

Even then there was concern that they might be spotted. One of Frank's errands might bring him to Whitefish Lake. There was no way of telling, really, where he might pop up in Algonquin Park.

So a ruse had to be organized for that Friday. Something that would keep Frank at home. Friends of Frank's daughter Adele agreed to provide it.

The friends — a family of four that Frank had never met — booked him for a guiding trip for the Saturday of the party. Said they would drive down from Cornwall the day before. Made arrangements with Frank to park their RV in his backyard for the night.

"We'll phone you when we get into Whitney," the man said. "Get directions to your house then."

"What time do ya think you'll be phonin'" asked Frank and the man said noon. If they got out of Cornwall all right. And depending on traffic. But he was aiming for noon.

He called shortly before two p.m.

"What took ya so long?" asked Frank.

"It was further than we thought," said the man. "But we're here now. How do we get to your home, Frank?"

"Where are you exactly?"

"One of the main intersections, I'd say," and the man started to describe where he was standing. Frank didn't pick up on "main intersection" right away but it didn't take him long after that to see there was a problem.

"You're at the traffic lights by the sportin' goods store?"

"Yes."

"There's no traffic lights in Whitney."

"What?"

"Ain't no sportin' goods store either."

"That's impossible Frank. I'm standing right here."

"What's the name on the sportin' goods store?"

"Sharpley's"

"Are you kiddin' me?"

"No. That's what it says. Sharpley."

"Holy Jeepers. You're in Huntsville."

"What?"

"You've' driven right through the Park."

"Of course we've driven through the Park! Adele said you were just outside the gates."

"Just outside the East Gate. Not the West Gate."

"Oh."

Frank rubbed his brow and counted to ten. He wasn't going to be able to take his eyes of these people for even a second when they were in the bush tomorrow.

"How far back is it to your place?" the man asked.

"It's a bit more'n an hour. Just turn around and come back."

"All right. We'll phone you when we get there."

"Right on."

———◆———

Frank went back to watching television. Working on a word puzzle. Going to his sunroom from time to time to grind Chaga. Back to the television. He hated being home in the afternoon.

The man called shortly before four.

"Sorry, Frank. We were getting hungry so we stopped for a late lunch."

"That's all right," Frank lied. "You're just 'round the corner now. I'll put on a pot of coffee."

"Great. We're bringing you some lunch."

"Don't need to do that."

"It's the least we can do. And honestly, this is some of the best barbecued chicken I've ever had."

Again, it didn't register right away. Frank was starting to give directions from the Mad Musher, or the Algonquin Lunch Bar, or Chris's Pizza Parlour — these being the three restaurants in Whitney that were open on the weekend — when he stopped and said:

"Barbecued chicken?"

"Yes. It's great. You must eat here all the time."

"What's the name of the restaurant?"

"The name of the restaurant? It's the Dixie Lee, Frank."

Frank began to wonder if this family could be trusted in a canoe.

"Jeepers. You still ain't in Whitney."

"What?"

"You're in Barry's Bay."

"No. That's impossible."

"Dang right it's impossible. How in the world did you miss Whitney?"

"Frank, you said it was the first town once you're past the East Gate. I'm standing in the first town past the East Gate."

"No you ain't. You're standing in Barry's Bay!"

The man thought for a minute.

"Hold it. You aren't talking about that gas station and gift shop right by the East Gate, are you?"

"Holy Jeepers, are you freakin' ... " and then Frank stopped talking. Not sure at all what to say next.

"Sorry," the man mumbled. "We'll turn around right now. How far is it?"

"It's fifty-five kilometres."

"We'll be there right away "

———◆———

The family arrived shortly after six. A man, woman, and two young boys. Bringing a bucket of Dixie Lee Chicken.

They had spent the day in Barry's Bay, talking to Adele by phone and tracking the progress of the convoy on its way to Algonquin Park. When the last RV pulled into Whitefish Lake they showed up at Frank's with the barbecued chicken.

The family seemed all right when they got there, which surprised Frank. He wasn't expecting much from people who could miss Whitney and end up in Huntsville, then back-track and miss Whitney so bad a second time they ended up in Barry's Bay.

He had been thinking of hiding the sharp knives.

———◆———

The next morning they headed out early. Frank took them to Rock Lake, where they could troll for lake trout a few hours, then switch over to bass. The family had two young boys and they would enjoy bass fishing.

Sure enough the lake trout fishing was slow. One small splake on the second pass and then nothing for the next two hours. Mid-morning they switched to bass, Frank bringing out the casting rods and spinners, anchoring the boat by a culvert nearly hidden by cat-tails and bulrushes. They started catching fish right away.

It was mostly all rock bass but the man caught a nice smallmouth late in the morning, his wife a bigger one a few minutes later, and although those were the only two they caught they seemed happy with that.

Frank cooked a shore lunch with one of the smallmouth bass and by two p.m. they were back at the boat launch. The man checked his phone for messages when they were in Frank's van, something he had yet to do that day.

Right after that he asked Frank if they could see some of the sights in Whitney.

"A sight-seeing tour? Of Whitney?"

"Yes. We'd quite like that."

So Frank took them to the trestle bridge over one arm of Galeairy Lake. The Couples Resort, where they drove through the grounds waving at people walking around in bathrobes. Down a gravel road to an unofficial picnic spot on the Madawaska River that everyone called Rosie's Cozy, one of the boys asking why it would have a name like that and his mother telling him not to ask so many questions.

They visited the Men Wah Tay gift shop. Opeongo Outfitters. Took a drive down Paradise Road because one of the boys had seen a street sign and liked the name. The man kept checking his phone as they drove, asking to visit more and more places.

Frank was down to wondering if it was too early to go to the dump and see if any black bears were around, when the man suddenly turned off this phone, looked at Frank and said:

"Shouldn't we be heading home?""

———◆———

It had taken them all day to get the house ready. There were balloons hanging from the cedar trees and the fence around the vegetable garden. There were banquet tables set up in the back yard, more than a dozen of them, pushed together to form a line of tables that could seat more than fifty people.

There were streamers and Japanese lanterns, a fire-pit some of the men had made earlier in the day. By mid-afternoon there was a pig turning on a spit and clay crock-pots filled with baked beans and five-meat-stew standing in the embers.

Children's paintings were taped to walls throughout the house. Stick-figure etchings of Frank fishing from a canoe. Brightly coloured murals from the older children with trees and blue-dollop lakes, speckled trout, Frank and Marie eating a shore lunch.

The number eighty was emblazoned on just about every picture. Most also had the words "Poppa" or "Poppy" writ-ten somewhere.

The RVs and campers and pickup trucks had all been moved from Whitefish Lake and parked in a line along the rear of Frank's backyard, where he wouldn't see them when he first drove in. Most of the vehicles had balloons taped to an antenna and streamers across the windshield. One camper had two large speakers on the roof and music had been playing throughout the afternoon. Kitty Wells, Hank Williams. Hank Snow.

Adele had warned people to be careful about the music. If her father came home and heard rock 'n' roll the party would be ruined. If he heard Billy Ray Cyrus he wouldn't bother stopping.

When everyone was alerted that Frank was on his way, they went and hid. All but one.

The decorations and preparations were on the inside of the cedar hedge and if all went as planned, Frank would drive right through before he knew what was happening. Which is what happened. Drove right in and saw her standing there in his driveway, wearing a bright red party dress.

Frank walked over to her.

"Hello Saralyn."

"Hello Poppa. Happy birthday."

"Did you do all this?"

"Some of it."

"Where is everyone?"

"They're hiding. Do you want to find them? I know where they are."

"I think we should."

The young girl held out her hand for Frank to grab. He clutched his great-granddaughter's hand and she led him toward his home.

"Come on," she said. "We've been waiting for you a long time."

———◆———

The second party was a few days later. Again, still before his actual birthday. A much smaller affair this time.

Frank had been working at Arowhon that day. Guiding in the morning. Unofficially overseeing the construction of a new swim dock in the afternoon. ("Do ya believe those kids been workin' on that for three days?")

He was on his way back to Whitney, walking to his van, when Theresa Pupulin, the general manager at Arowhon, came to find him. She said there was something Frank needed to look at before he left. Then she started heading to the games room, a stand-alone cabin not far from the lake.

As they walked Frank thought it was about time they did something with the games room. It was a good log cabin with an unobstructed view of the lake but it didn't get used much anymore. He wondered if shuffleboard tables were quite the draw they had once been.

When he walked into the games-room people started laughing and singing "Happy Birthday." A lot of people. The camp counselors he had been teasing most of the summer were there. Most of the maintenance and housekeeping staff. The clients he had taken fishing that morning were there as well, having heard about the party from Theresa and asked if they could come.

Sitting on the shuffleboard table was a cake burning with candles and a frost-icing outline of Frank's face. A pastry chef had thought of the idea and done an admirable job. Frank's nose would be three slices easily.

Frank blew out the candles, people cheered and then everyone started to pat him on the back and leave. Frank stood there with a cake server in his hand wondering what was happening. Theresa came up to him, put her arm around his shoulder and said:

"That cake's for later, Frank. There's something else you need to do for me first."

She took him by the arm and led him out the games room. As they walked under the pine toward the lake Frank remembered being in Arowhon a long time ago, someone holding his arm that day as well. He showed up drunk looking for Dominique. To borrow money probably. He couldn't remember.

But his brother was guiding and they threw him out. Two large waiters pinned his arms and jerry-marched him to his car, Eugene bringing up the rear, telling Frank he didn't want to see him back there unless he was with his brother.

Forty years later, Eugene was the one who phoned Frank to ask if he could start guiding at Arowhon. He had seen

Frank with great grandaughter Saralyn

Frank's book at a store in Huntsville and wanted Frank to know two things: He liked the book. Second, a story on Frank Kuiack was about the last thing he ever expected to see in a bookstore in Huntsville.

Frank had done well for himself, Eugene said and it would be nice to have him working at the resort as a guide. They had a lot of good trout lakes around Arowhon. Frank wouldn't need to go far. Eugene had read in the book that he wasn't doing any more overnight guiding.

Frank thought for a minute and then said:

"You got Burnt Island."

Eugene laughed so hard he started coughing. He was in his late 80s by then but remembered how every good guide he knew as a boy kept Burnt Island Lake as their back-up plan; for when they absolutely needed to catch trout before heading back to Arowhon in time to hear the dinner bell.

"Yes," Eugene said, when he had recovered enough to speak, "We got Burnt Island, Frank."

The first clients from Arowhon called him two days later. That would have been ten years ago. Frank kept walking toward the lake, over the spot where fishing guides used to pitch their tents every spring. He had no idea where they were heading.

———◆———

Then Theresa turned toward the dining hall. Frank slowed his pace without being aware of it and Theresa leaned her head in to say:

"You need to have dinner before you can eat cake, Frank."

"Nah. Nah Theresa. Look what I'm wearin'."

"I wouldn't want you looking any other way."

Before he knew it Frank was through the front doors. Something that had never happened before. To him or any other guide. Fishing guides were not allowed in the dining room at Arowhon Pines Resort. Never had been. The best

Frank with Theresa at Arowhon

ones, the most favoured ones, might get into the kitchen. If a client invited you, a guide could sit on the verandah and see into the dining room.

But no guide had ever been inside that room.

Theresa walked to a maître d', who bowed deeply, shook Frank's hand and said his table was ready.

"My table?"

"Yes sir. If you'll just follow me please."

A part of Frank felt like running right then. Every person in the dining hall was staring at him. A cigarette he had hastily butted outside the dining room was stuck behind one ear. But the maitre d' was in front of him, Theresa behind, and he was trapped.

So he kept walking. Trying not to stare at the people eating dinner, drinking wine, people from far away, with small flags in the centrepiece of their table to show where they came from: German flags. British. Japanese. Australian. American.

It felt to Frank as though he were walking down a receiving line. Right to a table overlooking the lake. Next to the stone fireplace. A table for two that had been stripped and re-set for one.

The maître d' pulled back a chair and Frank sat down. When he was seated, Frank motioned for Theresa to lean down and he said:

"Theresa, this is real nice. But I don't belong here."

"Frank, this is exactly where you belong."

"No I don't. Look at your guests. I don't belong here at all."

Theresa stood straight and motioned to the maître d', who had gone back to his station but had kept his eyes on the general manager. He turned to grab something from the reception table.

"Most of these people know who you are, Frank. For

crying out loud, we've got a scrapbook about you in the lobby."

"That still don't mean I belong here."

"Don't talk for a minute Frank. Just watch."

Theresa stood back to let the maître d' pass. In his hands he carried two small objects. The first was a Canadian flag, perched on a small pedestal that he placed in the middle of the table. The second was a card he took carefully from the palm of his hand and slid into a birch-branch placeholder.

While he was doing this people in the dining room began to point at Frank. Before long it seemed everyone in the dining room was pointing at him. Then a man seated two tables away stood up, walked over to Frank and extended his hand.

"You're the Last Guide, aren't you?" said the man and Frank nodded slowly. Stuck out his hand.

"It's Frank," he said.

"It's a real honour to meet you, sir."

Then the man shook Frank's hand but didn't say anything else. Turned and went back to his table. Like he jumped up and thanked people all the time.

"Have a nice dinner, Frank," said Theresa and then she was gone back to work.

Frank sat there for several minutes, not believing where he was. In the dining room of Arowhon Pines Resort. Seated at the best table in the room. About to have dinner with people that not only knew him, but seemed to like him.

He wondered if it was like this for everyone who lived to a certain age. Stick around long enough and you'll arrive at the opposite end of everything.

Just before the first course was served Frank reached over to turn the placeholder around. These sat on each table. Fashioned from birch branches, with a saw-cut in one branch that let you slip in a card with the family name of the people sitting at the table. Where they were from. If it were a business function, there would be a title or occupation.

The card read: Frank Kuiack. Fishing Guide. Algonquin Park.

The next day Frank turned eighty.

Epilogue

We love the things we love for what they are.

— Robert Frost

✦ EPILOGUE ✦

Last day of trout season — The Madawaska Canoe Company — How to learn — One good thought to another

In 2015 the last day of trout season fell on September 26. It had been a glorious autumn until then in the Algonquin Highlands. The September days were bright, with a high-arcing sun and little wind. Still warm enough to dress in the clothes you had worn all summer, only the nights a little cooler.

The leaves on the soft maples and birch had already turned, but the oak and sugar maples were just beginning. The hills were yellow and gold with just hints of red. Most leaves were still on the tree.

But the night before Closing Day it started to rain and sometime that night the wind came back as well, stripping leaves from trees and splaying them across roads, walls and windows across Whitney.

Kevin Heinz awoke in his bedroom on Paradise Road and stared out the window, at fat drops of rain that rolled down the pane before pooling and then slipping away in a gush of water that made him think of creeks in the spring.

Heinz was thinking of taking a holiday that winter and travel brochures for Cuba were on his nightstand. He was

Frank in the dining room of Arowhon Pines Resort

thinking of Varadero, an all-inclusive resort on the beach. He had never taken a Caribbean holiday. Never gone south at all.

His second winter as a retired man was coming up and he thought he should give it a try. He rolled over, propped himself up on his elbow and started to read.

In a few minutes, though, he had trouble concentrating. Started to debate whether the rain was bad enough to stay inside today. He kept staring back and forth, from photos of white sandy beaches and thatched Daiquiri huts to the rain falling through the pine outside his window.

In a few minutes he put down the brochures and went to get dressed.

———◆———

Drago Dumancic awoke at the ambassador's residence on Rock Lake, looked out his window and decided to stay in bed.

The campground would be open another two weeks, until Thanksgiving weekend, although he and Nana were almost the last ones there. There were a couple of RVs that had been there most of the month, with fishermen who came and went throughout the week, but he suspected they would be gone come Monday.

After that it would just be the German couple from Brantford, who for several years had also stayed the full season.

He never liked leaving Algonquin Park on Thanksgiving. The view of Rock Lake from his camper was one on the things he was most thankful for in this world, so it was a strange day to leave. He and Nana had talked over the years about leaving earlier but had yet to get around to it.

He stared at the rain falling on Rock Lake. Falling heavily enough to strip leaves from the maples by the shoreline, yet not heavily enough to clear out the mist that sat atop the lake.

He couldn't figure out why that would be. Kept staring at the rain, which fell as though from one cloud to another. Drago between clouds. Warm in his sleeping bag. Watching.

A beautiful country, yes.

———◆———

Matt Fitzpatrick also awoke early, although not because of the rain. It had become his habit to start the day before the sun rose, one more change in his life that he considered a good one and so he kept with it.

He lay in bed staring at the bassinette the other side of the room. His son had slept through the night. The first time he had done that. Six months old and that was a good sign. His wife lay beside him, still asleep, and when Fitzpatrick rolled out of bed he was careful not to wake her.

Things had not gone as planned. Fitzpatrick wasn't sure if there was a single thing in his life he could point to and say: "Right there. I planned that."

His father's cancer had returned late last year. Just invaded his body. Stage four in no fewer than three internal organs. The penance of a dutiful son had not been enough to save him. He had passed away that spring.

His father's affairs were complicated, with various properties mortgaged to keep the canoe company afloat, something no one knew about at the time. The Madawaska Bait and Tackle shop got caught up in all that and was forced to shut down.

Maybe not forced. Fitzpatrick could have kept it going. Just didn't seem worth the effort, with his dad no longer there. He had started working at the Couples Resort.

When the lawyers and bankers and tax people were finished there wasn't much left to his dad's estate. A half-dozen canoes and an old RV, which Fitzpatrick had driven back from Ottawa the week before.

Not as planned. Although as he reached down to pick up his son he wasn't thinking of complaining. Things had turned out all right in other ways.

He walked to the bedroom window, rocking his son in his arms, and once there stared out at the rain. His dad's RV needed mechanical work and Fitzpatrick had put it up on blocks. In the rain it looked like something abandoned, like the stone fences you ran across on the Opeongo Line sometimes, hidden under bramble and chockberry bushes, so far in the middle of nowhere you wondered what the fences could possibly have been protecting.

Through the falling rain Fitzpatrick could just make out what his dad had stenciled on the side of the RV: Madawaska Canoe Company. Established 2008.

———◆———

Frank sat in his living room with a hot cup of Nescafe coffee warming his hands. The wind had shifted since he woke an hour ago, coming from the north-west now. It was always a bad sign when wind shifted on you during a storm. Meant the storm was sticking around awhile. Not going to blow itself out standing in just one place.

His Woods rucksack was packed and waiting by the basement stairs. Frank had corded down a couple tarps to the top of the pack, but that had been his only concession to the weather. The pack bulged with the frying pan and cooking utensils he would need for a shore lunch.

He took one last look around his kitchen, butted his cigarette, grabbed his pack and headed downstairs. Outside it was still dark. He threw his gear into the van, turned on the heater and backed out the driveway.

The summer traffic was gone and his was the only vehicle on the highway. A lot of the campgrounds in Algonquin Park were already closed. He made the turn onto Highway

60 and a few minutes later was in the Park.

He was on his way to Little Joe Lake, where his last clients of the year, a Japanese couple staying at Arowhon, would be waiting for him. Assuming they still wanted to go out in weather like this.

It was the same weather in Ottawa that day. I sat at my desk and stared out my study window, at a steady rain that was stripping leaves from a row of hardwood trees the other side of the street. There was enough water rolling down the street to capture objects that drifted past my window: leaves, crumbled coffee cups, twigs and pine needles.

Frank's guidebook sat on my desk. Ready for me to drive up to him the following week.

That morning I read through the twelve lessons one last time and decided, put together, they came pretty close to what Frank said four years ago should be in a good guidebook: "Practical stuff people can use. Not the stupid stuff."

It also seemed close to what I had gone searching for at the same time. Frank's view of the world. Put the lessons together and this is what he's saying:

Take care of yourself. You're the best person to do that job, so don't rely on others.

Competition is good. It keeps life interesting and fun. Maybe that's the reason competitive people often life longer: they have been enjoying themselves.

You need to belong somewhere to find true happiness. You never find it on the road.

You need to love not only the people in your life, but everything else too. Otherwise love runs out on you

When you find something you love doing, keep doing it. Even if you disappoint people who think it is time for you grow up, keep doing what you love.

Keep an open mind. You never know when it's time to go bass fishing.

Frank on Head Lake

Those were the main lessons, and as I re-read the guide-book I felt like a student about to hand in a final paper and say goodbye to a favourite professor.

The night before it had even come to me, at last, how Frank had acquired that worldview. The trick that held everything together. It was the way he had learned.

We only have three ways to learn, to gain knowledge in this world. We are given some. At birth, we know how to suckle, how to gain a parent's attention.

After that we are taught. By parents, teachers, employers, governments; any and all institutions, any and all religions, philosophies and mission statements. "Learned knowledge" this is called. Or "book learnin" as Huck Finn might have called it.

The third form of knowledge comes from personal experience. From what we have discovered on our own, without the aid of others, without being taught, commanded or instructed. This is experiential knowledge. And if it is not the sum total of what Frank knows, it is certainly the bedrock.

So what happens when you look upon the world not in a way that has been taught you or presented you, but in the way you have found it?

Remarkable things, in my opinion. Sitting on my desk were four years worth of field notes.

———◆———

The couple was waiting on the verandah of the dining room when Frank arrived. Wearing yellow slickers and pants. Ready to go.

They were from Tokyo, in their mid-30s, spoke good English and as Frank loaded the canoe they told him they had never gone fishing.

"Never?"

"Never," they laughed. Never once considered it. But two nights ago they had been sitting in the lobby of Arowhon and had come upon a scrapbook of newspaper stories about Frank. The lakes and rivers in the photos looked just like the ones in the travel brochures that brought them to Canada.

They wanted to go fishing.

The couple kept talking when they were in the canoe, something Frank normally didn't like but they weren't complaining about the weather so he let them go. Talking and asking him all sorts of questions about fishing.

When they reached the portage into Burnt Island the couple watched with their mouths open as Frank put the canoe on his back and started walking. Something he didn't need to do as he had two canoes already hidden at Burnt Island, but he knew the couple would like to see it and he didn't mind showing them.

When they were on the water he gave them a quick lesson on trolling, explaining the importance of action, set out line for them, so they would be fishing at the right depth.

Thirty minutes later the woman caught a fish. Her line bowed nicely when she set the hook and after that she was screaming and yelling as though she was seated on a roller-coaster.

It was a small laker and when Frank brought it into the boat the couple stared at the fish with a curiosity that seemed comical to him, until he realized they had never seen trout before and that would explain it. If he were in Japan seeing something marvelous for the first time he'd probably look the same way.

"That's trout?" asked the woman.

"Lake trout. You can tell by the vee in its tail," and Frank showed her. Almost as though scripted it was the man who caught the next fish. A nice pound-and-a-half speckle, giving the man a good fight, the speckles on the belly flashing in the sun when Frank lifted it out of the water.

The couple pointed at the colourful dots and Frank said that was right, this was a different kind of trout.

LESSON TWELVE
Why You Should Fish: Part Two

"People ask me all the time why I kept guidin'. Some people don't understand it. Think it's strange.

"I tell 'em it ain't as strange as they think. Long as there were people willin' to pay me to take 'em out, why wouldn't I go? An' there were always some people. Not a lot some years, but always some.

"An' we're talking about fishin'. Don't forget that. Why does anyone want to fish? I've seen every kind of fisherman I guess there is to see, so I know every reason.

"Some people just like being out there. On a lake in Algonquin [Park]. Those people, they got binoculars out prit' near as soon as we leave the dock ... always have a Canoe Routes of Algonquin Park map with 'em somewhere.

"Other people just want to relax. Don't care much if we catch fish. These people practically nod off on the boat trip back.

"Some people want the fillets I give 'em at the end of the day. Wanna see a moose. Wanna see a good speckle.

"One guy hired me 'cuz he was datin' a girl that liked to fish but he didn't know how to do it and he figured he better learn. She musta been a real good-lookin' girl 'cuz that guy was in a right panic.

"I must 'a seen every reason out there for fishin'. (I fish) 'cuz I like it. Don't know if it needs to get more complicated 'n that. I like to fish.

"Why would you quit anything you like?"

THE
LAST GUIDE'S
GUIDE

An hour later they had their stringer filled and Frank took them for a shore lunch. The couple could have eaten every fish they caught that morning, so hungry were they, so delighted were they with the fried fish, both of them telling Frank they had eaten fish and chips before, but this fish was different, Frank being polite and saying nothing, although he did wonder what it would be like if the only fish you ever ate was frozen or caught yesterday. Wondering if he would bother.

They were back at Arowhon by two o'clock. Right on schedule. Although Frank didn't get away as quickly as planned. The couple wanted photos. Them with Frank. Them with trout. Each with Frank. Each with trout.

After they had done all that they paid him, tipped him and it was the woman who told Frank they had been in Canada two weeks, would be flying home from Toronto the next day, but this would be the highlight of their vacation. What they had come to Canada hoping to find.

"Now this," she said, pointing at a photo of Frank she had just taken; Frank smiling and smoking a cigarette, holding a string of trout, "is not like home."

——◆——

That night Frank had trouble sleeping. Which happened sometimes after a good fishing trip, one where the client was happy and had tipped well. Frank was pretty sure the couple would go home and tell stories to their friends and family about what they had done that day.

After doing it for seventy-two years Frank still wasn't sure what he liked most about guiding. The cash the Sports put in his hands at the end of the day. Or the small-child shouts and laughs they made when they caught fish.

Money or joy. He still hadn't decided.

With trout season finished he would give himself a day off tomorrow. Maybe half a day. Still lots of work to do before he headed to Cornwall for Christmas. He took his

A beautiful fish

last cigarette of the night from his pack, lit it with a Zippo lighter, and looked around his living room.

He stared at the framed photos hanging on the wall next to the television, including the only known photo of his mother and father standing together. The stuffed badger his brother-in-law gave him years ago, after Frank's sister had refused to have the animal in her house. The speckle trout above the television.

Seven-pounds-three-ounces and that fish looked as beautiful today as it did the day he pulled it from Source Lake. Opening Day 1990. Ice still on the lake and that fish had jumped right through it. An explosion of ice and water he had never seen before or since.

The fish had the burnished greens and dark reds of a good speckle trout. The colours reminded Frank of hardwood forests in autumn; or liquor bottles inside a glass case, when the sun hits the glass just right and the colours explode. Nearly thirty years sober, but some things stay with you.

That trout was a beautiful thing. Made Frank think of other beautiful things. Maybe every beautiful thing in the world and maybe that's how it worked, one good thought leading to another, like water moving down pools in a creek. No way you could stop it even if you wanted.

As he tried to sleep that night Frank wondered if it would be the same for the couple from Japan. Would they be happy twenty-five years from now, when they looked at the photos they had taken that afternoon? Just how far could a good memory ripple?

Frank thought about it for quite awhile, tossing and turning in his bed, deciding just before he fell asleep that it was possible. There might be no end to it.

About the Author

Ron Corbett is a journalist, broadcaster and author living in Ottawa. His columns and features for the *Ottawa Citizen*, *Ottawa Sun* and *Ottawa Magazine* have won numerous awards, including two National Newspaper Awards. He is married to photojournalist Julie Oliver and admits to being a poor, or transitioning, fisherman. This is his seventh book.

Acknowledgments

The Last Guide's Guide was only completed with the assistance of many people living in the Algonquin Highlands, in particular: Kevin Heinz, Matt Fitzpatrick, Theresa Pupulin, and Drago Dumancic.

Jack Mihell remains a good sport fisherman and a good sport. As do the regulars of the Twin E restaurant (which, sadly, shut down after this book was completed).

I would like to thank my family, Julie, William, Hailey, Tara and Dylan for understanding that the final days of any writing project are rarely pretty. Julie gets a double thank you, for once again photographing Frank in a way that is honest and memorable.

I would like to thank George D'Aoust for his support and encouragement in the writing of this book.

Magdalene Carson of New Leaf Publication Design cannot be thanked enough for her hard work and perfect understanding of how to visually tell a good fishing story. Scott Sigurdson, a friend for many years, did just as wonderful a job with the cover design.

I would like to thank anyone involved with the running, maintaining or preserving of Algonquin Provincial Park. The Park is a treasure that needs to be passed on, generation to generation.

Lastly, I would like to thank Bob Dylan, for no specific reason other than it always strikes me as a good thing to do. This time it is for the *Basement Tapes*.